Coinage & Conflict

BY HENRY POLLAK

Coinage & Conflict

BY HENRY POLLAK

THE COIN & CURRENCY INSTITUTE, INC.

P.O. Box 1057, Clifton, N.J. 07014

(973) 471-1441 • E-mail: coincurin@aol.com

Coinage & Conflict

CONTENTS

Acknowledgment iii
Introduction iv

Part 1: Legends in Gold, Silver and Bronze

The Tortoise Who Learned to Walk 2
The Roman Propaganda Machine 4
Blood, Sweat, Tears and Inflation 8
A Flight to the West 10
Of Myths and Morals 12
A Modest Huntress and An Immodest Lady 14
The Coin Inspired by Ben Franklin 16
An Eagle Eye — On War or Peace? 18
"Value Me As You Please" 20
"Millions for Defense" 22
A Fugitive From New Haven 24
Cartoon Tales 26

Part 2: Coinage, Conflict — and God

An American Debate 32
Greek Gods on the Wing 34
Rome, the Republic and the Rise of the Caesars 36
The Descent of the Gods 38
The Circumcision War 44
The Death March of the Gods on the Road to Constantinople ... 50
The Throne of Jesus 54
Defender of the Faith 58
Dutch Courage 64
Paradise Removed 66

Appendix 70

Pages 2 - 9, 16-19 Graphics by Charles Davidson

Copyright © 2001, Henry Pollak
All rights reserved

Acknowledgments

I would like to thank those who have helped me write this book. Going back to the early beginnings, it was "Jocko" Reardon, a great teacher at the Taft School in Watertown, Connecticut, who inspired my first interest in the subject of history in 1937. Five men, who were recognized as leaders of the numismatic world contributed their time and thoughtful comments during the years from 1950 to 1960 to educate a young man in his 30s who, at that time, had the inclination, but not the surplus cash, to become an important client. These were Eduard Ganz of Numismatic Fine Arts, Leo Mildenberg of Bank Leu Zurich, Richard Picker, a specialist on colonial America, and Harvey and Morton Stack of Stack's Coin Company. These men were my professors. I could not have written this book without them.

In preparing my text, I would like to thank Ron Carran for his imaginative work in providing the graphics and background for most of this book. Tom Muller provided all but a few of the professional photographs of my coins, with Charles Davidson providing some of the photos for the early chapters, along with ideas for the graphics.

Debbie Ardino was the one to follow up on 1,001 details with energy, accuracy and persistence, while maintaining her sense of humor.

I am very appreciative that Jill and Michael Charnaud of Newdigate, England allowed me to photograph and use the magnificent handmade interpretation they have of the Bayeux Tapestry which has meaning for their family.

One chapter in this book entitled "Dutch Courage" is included only because of the very valuable advice and pictures received from Joseph R. Lasser, a specialist in the field of numismatics, represented by the currency in this chapter. I am very grateful to him for the help that made this chapter possible.

During the Winter of 2001, when we required additional authentic photographs of the old New England scene as background for our colonial coins, we called on our friend Bob Hopewell of Wolfeboro, New Hampshire, who waded waist-deep into the snow to get us the pictures we needed. We thank him very much. Spinks provided us with a photograph from their catalogue of a Mary Stuart testoon — a coin we needed to tell our story but did not own. And Coin World gave us permission to use photographs of cartoons from their issue of July 14, 1965. We appreciate both companies' willingness to allow us to use these materials.

Through the years, I have disposed of the coins in my collection to individuals who now provide them an appropriate home. This book perpetuates the collection for me. Above all, I thank Jean, my editor and chief, who spent hours reviewing the text — even presuming at times to criticize it — and who helped to add the extra judgment and balance we all need when we're talking about history.

Henry Pollak

Introduction

Coinage was developed about 2500 years ago as a convenient alternative to barter. The very word "pecuniary" comes from the Latin word "pecus," meaning cattle which was one medium of exchange, along with corn, grain and other tangibles. We can only imagine the complexity of each transaction in which traders had to know the condition and age of each cow, the number of rows of corn and the varying standards of each locality in which they were doing business. By the time of Genesis, about 2000 BC, we know that there was at least a common standard of measure — a specific weight of precious metal: "Abraham weighed to Ephron the ... 400 shekels of silver current money with the merchant." Even so, the metal had to be carefully weighed for each transaction, a burdensome and time-consuming procedure.

The first coins were made by engraving a die which was set into an anvil. A fixed weight lump of softened or molten metal was set into the anvil and struck with a punch. Alternately, the engraving could be made on the punch instead of on the anvil die. In due course, there were two sides engraved — the anvil side being the obverse, and the punch side being the reverse of each coin.

It is these engravings which provide the story of this book.

A molten flow of gold, silver and bronze has been variously molded, hammered, struck and cast to become fixed weight discs onto which specific images have been made to appear. In some ways these images may be considered miniature statues because they were often given as much thought by the rulers who created them as any statue in their realm.

A Greek or Roman ruler wanted to pay his soldiers in a currency of indisputable value and, therefore, a specific weight of precious metal. However, coins were much more than lumps of fixed weight metal. They represented sometimes the image of a god, sometimes the face of the emperor, and sometimes the symbol of an entire people (this might be a bird or other creature associated with their history — or in the case of Rome, a wolf suckling the children who became its mythical founders).

The coin, having two sides, an obverse and reverse, could of course tell two stories, which it often did very effectively. One side might identify the ruler, and the other his powers as a deity:

OB (obverse) — Emperor Tiberius
RX (reverse) — The highest priest

One side might identify a military leader, and the other side his close military ally and (in this case) his lover.

OB — Antony
RX — Cleopatra

One side might represent an entire nation, and the other side its philosophy as in the case of the American continental dollar which was partly designed by Benjamin Franklin:

OB – The linked states of the Union
RX – The Puritan ethic of hard work

Visual images were important, of course. But so were the legends which identify the leaders and their causes. Coins were the medium of exchange, but they were also a form of expression setting out the goals of a particular society at its time in history. Each coin represents a static view — a point of history at a specific time and place. However, just as a young child connects dots to make a definable picture, we can link the points of history to show change and development. The coinage changed in response to conflict, and the story of conflict is often reflected in the coins themselves. There were conflicts between rulers. Who had won and who had lost? The coins let the people know, just as they tell us today. There were conflicts of religion — the struggles of the Jews and Christians against their pagan overlords and the long conflict in England between the Protestant Reformation and the establishment. There were conflicts of ideas as seen in the new American republic. It was always the victors who won the right to strike the coins of the realm and the new victors often wanted to send a new message. These messages of change and conflict have been well preserved for us to read and understand — an enduring history written on the coinage of the ages.

Part 1
LEGENDS IN GOLD, SILVER AND BRONZE

The Tortoise Who Learned to Walk

*I*n the 7th Century B.C., the people of the Greek island of Aegina, about ten miles offshore in the Aegean Sea, came up with a remarkable and origi-

nal idea. Because their population could not produce enough on their small island to support themselves, they needed to take advantage of their special skills as sailors and traders. So they turned their island into a Hong Kong of its time and became a great trading center, sending their ships as far away as Egypt across the Mediterranean. In the course of trading with that country, they discovered an active market for silver.

G-1-ff (AR)
Aeginan Sea Turtle
about 600 B.C.

Aegina did not have its own silver mines so these resourceful people imported the precious metal from another island nearby and then converted it into the first silver coins the world had seen — featuring on one side the simple figure of a sea turtle, which was the badge of their island, and on the other side only the mark of the punch which struck the coin.

Wherever their currency was accepted, this island people would be identified. In our terms, they were using their logo to advertise their homeland and their products. For 200 years these coins were well known throughout the Greek Archipelago as "Turtles." We know that they succeeded in finding their market in Egypt because a number of hoards of these Aeginan "Turtles" have been found in that country.

Unhappily for the people of Aegina, a rival power was coming to the fore in nearby Greece — the Athenians, who would not only become dominant in trade and intellect, but who would also rule the Aegean Seas.

CHAPTER 1

Currency is based on trust and credibility. Now that Athens controlled the waters around Aegina, a sea turtle no longer seemed appropriate. The people of Aegina retreated strategically, but they did not leave the field. Their unique coinage was reissued about 400 B.C., still featuring the badge of the island of Aegina, but now the turtle had become a land tortoise marked with identifying square patterns on his shell. History had been written in durable silver on the back of a tortoise.

The people of Greece had a superstition that the tortoise was a creature of the devil. Whether for that reason or for more rational ones, Aegina never regained its former place in Mediterranean trade.

G-1-f (AR)

Aeginan land tortoise about 400 B.C. (enlarged 6x)

The Roman Propaganda Machine

The Murder of Caesar

When President Kennedy was assassinated, the world knew it within hours and millions of people had actually seen the assassination on television. In Roman times, the populace was, of course, without any such form of mass communication. The Roman rulers knew, however, that they had to have a way of reaching the people in their far-flung dominions. They had to feed them the news — both truth and propaganda. One of the key things they wanted the Roman people to know, especially in the midst of their many civil wars, was the identity of the winner — who was their supreme ruler.

The solution was found in the coinage of the realm — a product with a message that was difficult to erase. Most important of all, it was delivered into the hands of those to whom the message was most important, the Roman army. The propaganda became the paycheck.

Marcus Junius Brutus and his co-conspirator, Cassius, knew how to use this tool. They noted that Julius Caesar, as Proconsul and ruler of republican Rome, had authorized a coin bearing his own likeness. No Roman coin had ever before this been struck bearing the image of a living ruler, and this confirmed to the Roman aristocracy that Caesar had the aim of becoming their first emperor. The ancient belief was that a living portrait was an image of a god and, at least in the view of Brutus and his party, those who presumed to be gods must be destroyed. The coin appeared on the streets of Rome in February 44 B.C. and one month later on March 15th, Julius Caesar was assassinated in the Senate at Rome at the hands of Brutus and his co-conspirators.

Brutus became Caesar's successor as the republican ruler of Rome. He determined at first to avoid Caesar's mistake; he would issue no coin bearing his own likeness. His early coins featured among others the head of Liberty, just as American coins did 1800 years later. Eventually, however, he was forced to change this policy because of the doubts about his rule and the powerful coalition being mobilized to overthrow him.

Marc Antony, a general and cohort of Caesar's, had stirred the Roman populace by reading them their dead leader's generous will in their favor and then joined with Lepidus and Octavian, Caesar's nephew, to form an effective triple alliance against the conspirators. Because of this triumvirate's constant military pressure, even the mint which struck the coins had to be moved periodically, and Brutus finally decided that he, himself, must be seen as the personal leader and embodiment of liberty. He represented this on a silver denarius which showed the people and troops, not only who their ruler was,

R-1-a (AR)
Denarius
OB: The head of Julius Caesar

CHAPTER 2

R-1-aaa (AR)
RX: Liberty cap and two daggers underneath which appears the date EID MAR (March 15th)

R-1-aaa (AR)
Denarius
OB: Head of Brutus (see Appendix)

but how he had achieved his role (by assassination) and the very date on which to celebrate this "glorious" occasion — the Ides of March, which is March 15th.

This was fine propaganda for its time, but no match for the power which the Triumvirate was mounting against Brutus. The ill-fated conspirators were finally defeated at Philippi, and Brutus killed himself in the year 42 B.C., the very year in which he had issued a coin bearing his portrait.

Now there was a new succession to power by the Triumvirate who had defeated Brutus, but there were, in fact, only two competitors for the ultimate control of Rome — Octavian and Marc Antony.

The Bondage of Antony and Cleopatra

Cleopatra, the inheritor of the Egyptian throne of Ptolemys, was, by all accounts, a remarkable woman. Though she lived for only 39 years, she ruled Egypt for 22 of those years. During that time, she learned the languages of all of her major near-East neighbors, including Syrian, Hebrew, Arabian and Parthian. Above all, she was a woman of such bewitching presence that she was able to make first Julius Caesar and then eight years later, Marc Antony, her paramours.

Much of what we know about the liaison between Antony and Cleopatra comes from Plutarch's *Life of Marcus Antonius*, some of which was based on the testimony of actual witnesses to the events of the time. Plutarch indicates that it was not her beauty so much as her presence and magnetism that drew men of vast power to her side. Shakespeare, who used Plutarch as his source, described her as follows:

> "Age cannot wither her, nor customs stale
> Her infinite variety. Other women cloy
> The appetites they feed, but she makes hungry
> Where most she satisfies …"

We come to see her as a scheming queen who sought not just to advance her personal cause but, above all, to secure her throne and her people with the rulers of Rome who represented the only super power of their day.

Marc Antony, as a member of the Triumvirate ruling Rome, represented that power in Egypt. His involvement with the voluptuous queen became a real problem for his two colleagues in Rome who were at that time being threatened by the rising naval power of General Pompey off the coast of Italy. Antony returned to Rome in order to help maintain his own and his associates' power. During several years' stay, he also married Octavia, the sister of his powerful colleague Octavian Caesar. This would surely have left him a secure place in Rome.

Once a treaty had been signed with Pompey, however, the force holding the Triumvirate together shattered. Antony, leaving both Octavia and Rome, returned to his Egyptian queen and the eastern empire he ruled with her. A separate power was being established within the Roman realm, and its coinage made clear how that power was being shared.

This coin was designed to show both the Roman and Egyptian armed forces how durable the link was between their two countries, with Marc Antony on the obverse and Cleopatra on the reverse of the same coin. Octavian, who was, after all, the nephew of Julius Caesar, was unable to let such a challenge pass. He descended on Egypt with both land and naval forces. Antony, an experienced and successful general, made the fatal error of meeting Octavian's challenge, not on land where he might have prevailed, but at sea in the battle of Actium, 31 B.C. His fleet had depended upon the support of Cleopatra's naval forces of 60 ships, but at the start of the battle, all of the Egyptian fleet left the scene. We have no explanation for this in history. Antony, linked to Cleopatra in coinage, also appeared to follow her in retreat. Immediately after his defeat, he fell on his sword and died.

R-6-f (AR)
OB: Antony

R-6-f (AR)
RX: Cleopatra

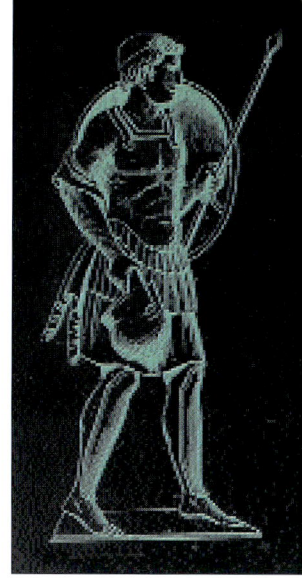

This was an act worthy of a now very secure Octavian who would in 27 B.C. rise to the throne as Augustus Caesar, the first emperor of Rome. His handsome portrait appeared on the coinage of his day with the words on the reverse of the coin, "OB CIVIS SERVATOS" — "on behalf of the citizenry served." The Romans were now ready for the heady days of empire and Augustus Caesar ruled them for forty years.

Octavian offered generous terms to Cleopatra, wishing for an end to conflict and stability within the boundaries of Rome. Cleopatra, however, realized that she would eventually be paraded before the mobs of Rome as a trophy, and unwilling to suffer such humiliation, she followed her love, Antony, in suicide.

In a final gesture, Octavian ordered that she should be buried next to Antony, and his own soldiers attended the funeral.

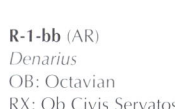

R-1-bb (AR)
Denarius
OB: Octavian
RX: Ob Civis Servatos

Blood, Sweat, Tears and Inflation

*I*n Paul Kennedy's *Rise and Fall of the Great Powers,* we find the repeated history of powerful nations which extend beyond their means and which allow their military spending in the end to undermine their economic base of survival. The United States in the early 1980s had to confront the fact that its burgeoning military budget (combined with other big government programs) was threatening its economic preeminence. Deficits were rising at an unacceptable rate. Fortunately, the Soviet Union — faced with exactly the same problem — collapsed before America did.

One of the historical early examples cited by Paul Kennedy was the empire of the Byzantines. The history of the rise and fall of one great power was clearly written in the gold of its coinage.

The Byzantine empire lasted 700 years under eight succeeding royal families. Its seat of its power was in Constantinople which considered itself not only the successor power to the Roman Empire, but also the center of Christian theocratic authority throughout the world — in competition with the Roman Church. Even after the Moslem Turks finally defeated the Byzantines and seized Constantinople in the 15th century, Byzantine culture remained the spiritual guidepost for the Eastern Orthodox (or Greek) Catholic Church which predominated throughout most of Eastern Europe.

Because the philosophy of the Byzantine rulers was a very conservative one, we can learn a great deal by observing the remarkably few changes in the nature of their gold coinage over the 700-year period. Considering that this was a regime which felt that its rock-like stability must be reflected in its coinage, these changes had to represent vast force. The very appearance of the gold coin of the Byzantines, the Solidus, illustrates a shallow linear portraiture, deliberately chosen to be different from the earlier and much more sculptured natural beauty of Greek and Roman coinage.

R-8-o (AV)
Solidus
OB: 717 AD
Theophilus

The Byzantine Solidus on which the entire currency was based was about the size of the American cent and twice its weight. It was designed to represent the state which considered itself heir to the Roman Empire and, as the only gold coinage in Europe, this imperial currency became the standard for Western Europe as well. The west could not afford a gold coinage in those times.

Currency of this status had to be endowed with special qualities of purity (called "shimaya") and with a highly uniform appearance, in order to give the impression of great stability. The gold was indeed pure during the early centuries, being 86-90% gold. To illustrate its buying power, one Solidus represented one day's salary of a government bureaucrat.

The change in the coinage started in the year 945 under Michael VII who was engaged in a struggle to preserve the last of Byzantium's Italian provinces. Though he did not succeed in that undertaking, he was a good financial manipulator and found a way to finance his military undertakings by debasing the Solidus, making it over 60% silver in a pale yellow "electrum" metal. The shape of the coin was also changed into a very thin concave shape called "scyphate" (cup-shaped).

CHAPTER 3

R-7-h (AV)
Nomisma
OB: Michael VII Solidus
(Scyphate)

These thin coins were much more subject to clipping — a technique of minutely trimming the edges and an easy way to steal gold. There was one other point: if one stacked these scyphate coins high enough, they would topple over. That should have been a prophetic warning to the leaders of the Byzantine.

In some respects the decline of the empire was beyond the control of its rulers because the two-front threats from the Latin west and from the Moslem east were constant and growing. Eventually this brought the militant Comneni dynasty to the throne to lead Byzantium through much of the 11th and 12th centuries. (There was one 22-year interregnum.) These were centuries of war and deterioration of the empire. The greatest military burden developed at the end of the 11th century when 300,000 fighting men gathered in Byzantium for the beginning of the first Crusade. These friendly troops did more to burden the empire than the opposing Turkish army.

With hundreds of thousands of Crusaders circulating through the Empire — troops who were foreign, far from their homes and restless — it was necessary to keep their payroll intact. These troops had to be paid in the only currency they recognized and there was just not enough gold to go around.

From 1081 to 1118 under Alexius I Comnenus the Solidus became 80-90% silver and the balance gold — almost the opposite of its original formulation. Around the year 1097, the same year as the beginning of the first Crusade, the Solidus was discontinued and replaced by the new scyphate coin, the Nomisma, which was just a continuation of Alexius I's scyphate, mostly silver coins, but it was time to recognize that they were no longer related to the original gold Solidus.

R-7-j (AV)
Nomisma
OB: Alexius I
(Scyphate) Nomisma

In 1204, at the end of the fourth crusade, the dynasty of the Comneni came to an end and was followed by an interim from 1204 to 1258 when the Latin church ruled. It was during this period that Constantinople was sacked — an event still recalled by the Greek Orthodox during Pope John Paul's visit to Greece in the Spring of 2001, at which time he was asked to seek forgiveness for an event which had occurred three-quarters of a millenium earlier. Michael VIII of the Paleolagus dynasty recaptured Constantinople and restored the Byzantine court in 1258 but he could not restore its glory. It was his son, Andronicus II, who struck the last gold coins of the Byzantines — a striking of poor quality (not pictured) featuring Mary praying on the obverse and the emperor on the reverse.

By then it was too late for prayer because, according to a chronicler of the time, "There was nothing in the imperial treasury but cobwebs and air."

A Flight to the West

During the 1930s, great artists like Toscanini and Marlene Dietrich left their native countries and fled west to escape tyranny. A generation later, Barishnykov turned his back on Russian communism to find a new home in the west. In the fifth century BC, there was another emigration of artists — a flight to the west which effected the very nature of our coinage. These emigrants were the skilled engravers of Greek coins who had been trained in Athens and Ionia. In 479 BC, an Athenian trained artisan, whom we know only by his initials AR, made dies to produce coins for the Queen Consort of Syracuse on the Island of Sicily. The people of Syracuse had never seen coins like this. They were considered small works of art.

Despite the Greek victory at Marathon about ten years earlier, the Persians were still considered to be a major threat throughout the Greek islands, and talented Greek engravers and other artisans continued to migrate to southern Italian towns like Thurii and to Syracuse in Sicily. Eventually, Syracuse came to be considered one of the great centers of Greek culture.

The coins made by these emigrant artisans have probably never been equalled. They represent on their obverse deeply sculptured and expressive portraits, and on their reverse, a great variety of scenes of racing chariots, animals, thunderbolts of Zeus and other representations of the gods.

G-3-ww (AE)
OB: Artemis (Diana)
RX: Zeus Thunderbolt

CHAPTER 4

G-3-yy (AE)
Anapes
OB: "**Heads**"
(see Appendix)

These engravers did not simply move to the west geographically. Far beyond that, they became the inspiration for the coinage of the western world. The mints which they established in southern Italy and in Syracuse were within easy reach of the Roman Republic as it expanded to the south during the third century BC. The output of these Greek centers became the models for Rome's great coinage.

It is an irony of history that when a small Greek town, Bezant, became Constantinople about 1000 years later, it created a totally different, flat and linear style for its coinage, often with portraits on both sides, in order to distinguish itself from the competing Roman currency, which ancient Greece had originally inspired.

The standard of ancient Syracuse with its sculptured "heads" and "tails" won out however. If you doubt that, look at the coins in your own pocket.

G-3-yy
Pegasus
RX: "**Tails**"

Of Myths and Morals

"The so called divinities of Olympics have not a single worshiper among living men. They belong now not to the departments of theology but to those of literature and taste. There they still hold their place ... for they are too clearly connected to the finest productions of poetry and art, both ancient and modern, to pass into oblivion."

Bullfinch's Mythology

To the ancient Greeks and Romans, the myths were indeed beyond theology. They were part of the everyday lives of the people. The ancients lacked means of communication which we take for granted and which provide diversion. They lacked television and movies. They did, however, have storytellers who thrived on telling tales like the following:

An all powerful king has a child by his mistress, and his enraged wife schemes to have the child killed.

or

The lovely daughter of a noblewoman is kidnapped by the head of the underworld and held hostage.

The ancient Greeks could follow such stories in their myths, sympathize with some of the players and hate others — and relate the stories to their own lives. Some of the stories are reflected in Greek coinage. The "all powerful king" of those times was the King of the Gods — Zeus. The jealous wife, his queen, was Hera, who sought to kill the mistress' infant by placing two large serpents in his crib. This infant, however, being no ordinary child, but Hercules, the son of Zeus, strangled the serpents with his bare hands. Hera continued to plague young Hercules, inflicting him with madness and tragedy, and to improve the chances of

CHAPTER 5

G-3-vv (AE)
OB: Zeus

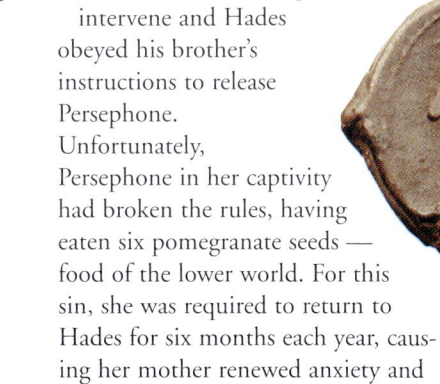

killing him, had a friendly king assign ten impossible and dangerous tasks to the young hero. The first of these tasks was to kill a monstrous lion with an impervious skin. Hercules strangled the lion and skinned it with the lion's own claws.

The "noblewoman" was Ceres, the goddess of all things that grow in the field, and protector of flowers. On one occasion, the earth opened up near her beautiful daughter Persephone and Hades, who was Zeus's brother and king of the lower world, emerged long enough to seize Persephone and bring her down into the depths with him. Ceres was so desperate in searching for her daughter that she neglected her duties. The crops of the world failed. Zeus was required to intervene and Hades obeyed his brother's instructions to release Persephone. Unfortunately, Persephone in her captivity had broken the rules, having eaten six pomegranate seeds — food of the lower world. For this sin, she was required to return to Hades for six months each year, causing her mother renewed anxiety and renewed neglect of her duties each fall and winter.

G-3-w (AE)
OB: Young Hercules
RX: Lion

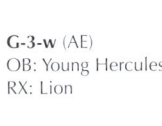

G-3-oo (AE)
OB: Persephone

A Modest Huntress and an Immodest Lady

R-6-b (AR)
RX: Diana

$\mathcal{B}$efore the third century BC, there was a great temple of Diana in Ephesus. Though the temple was destroyed, much of the rest of Ephesus can still be seen, including a two-story library and a house of prostitution.

The statues and images we still have of Diana show her as the goddess of the hunt, accompanied by the stags who pulled her chariot and her hunting dogs. We also have a coin which features the many-breasted Diana. This coin, however, glorifies Diana as a goddess of nature and nourishment, not lust. Diana the huntress was not only chaste, but vigilant in defense of her chastity.

On one occasion, a would-be suitor, also a hunter, followed her and her nymphs to a fountain where Diana chose to bathe. When Diana realized that she had been observed by this uninvited visitor, she splashed his head with water, turning him into a stag who was promptly devoured as prey by his own dogs. Though Diana was reputed to be quite beautiful, it is clear that she was well qualified to defend her virginal status.

CHAPTER 6

There is another famous instance of a lady who was seen unclothed, but this was her own choice. At the very end of the 18th century, Earl Leofric who was the Lord of Coventry, England, was subjecting the town to very high taxes at great cost to its citizens. His wife, Lady Godiva, appealed to him to relieve his subjects. Earl Leofric did not intend to reduce his income but, on the other hand, did not want to flatly turn down his wife. He replied that he would do just as she suggested if she would ride her white horse naked through the town. Lady Godiva took him up on the challenge and (somewhat protected by her very long locks) rode through the town while the citizens of Coventry all, by agreement, stayed indoors and averted their eyes. According to legend, all did but one; this was Tom the tailor, who was then struck blind, famous in history as Peeping Tom.

B-4-c (AE)
OB: Godiva
Half Penny

The Coin Inspired by Ben Franklin

When a new nation comes into being, much is written about what the founders did and how they thought. There is another way to tell that story — through the enduring sculptured images and legends on the coinage of the time. Because coins are dated, we can relate changes in government or its philosophy to a particular point in time.

We are not surprised to find that before the Revolution, the still loyal colonies continued to represent King George III on the obverse of the half penny with his crest shown on the reverse, as shown by the Virginia half-penny below.

That all changed following the Declaration of Independence. One of the most important pattern coins, the Continental Dollar, was probably struck in Philadelphia in 1776. Both its design and the mottos appearing on the coin were influenced by Benjamin Franklin and tell a story which we take for granted today, but which was in those monarchial times unthinkable except in the American colonies.

On the obverse, the names of the 13 original states are linked surrounding the legend which proclaims the necessary unity of these states if they are to replace the English King: "WE ARE ONE."

The reverse is equally symbolic of the new nation. There is a sun (Benjamin Franklin asked "Is it rising or setting?"). And there are symbols and

U-7-t (AE)
VA Half-Penny
OB: George III
RX: Crest

CHAPTER 7

legends representing the work ethic of the new nation. A sun dial relates to the Latin word *fugio* (I fly), which implies that if time flies, it had better not be wasted. The legend below the dial, "Mind your Business" does not tell the observer to butt out. Rather it says, in effect, "Watch your Nest Egg." These were good solid Yankee principles. This very important coin may have been authorized under a resolution which referred originally to paper currency. Because it was made of pewter — the common dinnerware metal on which so many of the Colonial Americans took their meals — it was clearly not worth a dollar. Therefore, it was probably used as a substitute for paper money only or as a pattern coin when originally issued.

We know that paper currency was issued with the same themes and was marked with a value of two-thirds of a dollar. A small number of these coins was struck in silver and may well have circulated as regular dollar currency.

Though the United States Mint did not strike coins until years later, the first coin issued under the authority of Congress was a "fugio" copper cent modeled precisely on the Continental dollar and dated 1787. These coins were first minted in New Haven from copper bands which held together French powder kegs used during the Revolutionary War.

U-7-kk (Pewter)
Continental Dollar

An Eagle Eye — On War or Peace?

A new nation requires not only the recognized symbols of state, but also a simple authority for all coinage. Because this would not happen in the United States until 1792, the country had to improvise, using all sorts of substitutes for national coinage. These included pattern coins and trade coins which were often imported from England or Ireland, but were also made in America. The value of these coins depended upon their weight and scarcity. There was also coinage issued by the individual states which was authorized by the Articles of Confederation which on March 1, 1781 specified that Congress would have the sole right to regulate and value coins struck under its authority.

While we do not know of state records which authorized the production of coins following the Revolution in New York State, there was a company in Newburgh, New York which established a "manufactory" called Machin's Mill. This mill produced copper coins for several of the new states and also, of course, for the home state of New York. One of these New York coins, the Excelsior, features the design on its obverse which became (and still is today) the New York State seal. The reverse of this coin features the American eagle with an olive branch of peace in its right claw and arrows in its left claw. The eagle is facing left in the direction of the arrows.

U-7-n (AE)
Excelsior copper

The state of Massachusetts established a mint in October of 1786. It is notable that even without a national coinage, there was an underlying common sentiment as to the themes to be represented such as the themes of liberty, nature, native life, justice and the American eagle which were represented in the coinage of the American states and formed the common basis of the later national coinage.

The obverse on the Massachusetts cent features an Indian, while the reverse features an American eagle closely similar to that used on the New York Excelsior copper. There is, however, a significant difference. Except for a few pattern pieces, which were probably never circulated, the eagle faces to its right, toward the olive branch of peace.

CHAPTER 8

U-7-ee (AE)
Massachusetts cent

This became the standard posture for the American eagle — one which was validated in a 1791 cent honoring George Washington, showing the first President on the obverse and on the reverse an American eagle. There are two versions of this reverse and both feature an eagle of peaceful intent.

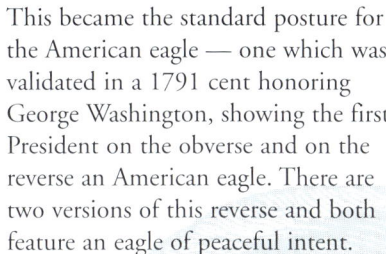

U-7-nw (AE)
George Washington cent

The Washington obverse, in combination with the eagle reverse of that 1791 coin, continues to this day. Consider the current U.S. quarter and you will see that the first President of the United States and the American eagle are still there. The eagle still glares to his right, but he gives no "claw signals." Both claws simply grasp a tree branch on which the national bird is standing, with no arrows and no olive branch. Modern American diplomacy is often ambiguous.

Current U.S. quarter

"Value Me As You Please"

The colonists of America had to be resourceful in many ways and one challenge affected the way they lived their lives every single day. Britain never sent any of its official currency and coinage to America. The colonists, therefore, had to find a way to live and trade effectively without any recognized system of money. Barter could involve fur skins, wampum beads — or even tobacco. Foreign coins had both a recognized value and a standard weight. The Spanish dollar, therefore, became a favorite among the early Americans and one Spanish real or "bit" was worth an eighth of a Spanish dollar. When we refer today to a quarter as "two bits," we are actually using a colonial term.

The entrepreneurs of the times were ready to take advantage of the severe shortage of small denominations. Many copper coins and tokens were produced in England and shipped to colonies in great variety and different degrees of authenticity. Because the need was so great, most of these coins found a welcome home in America. One particularly resourceful colonist decided that it would be worth his while to produce copper for coinage and other uses right in his home town of Granby, Connecticut. Samuel Higley, with a degree from Yale, was a doctor living in that town, but he had another occupation as a blacksmith and metallurgist. He arranged to purchase land on Copper Hill near Granby and started the production of copper of such fine quality that it could be used as an alloy for making gold. According to a Bowers and Merena catalogue of 1984, Dr. Higley was traveling to England in 1737 with a cargo of copper from his own mine on board and died during the voyage. His son, John Higley, became the owner of the mine and the dispenser of the copper tokens made from its fine quality metal. They were issued during the same year as his father's death, 1737.

These first coins featured a deer and the legend: THE VALUE OF THREE PENCE. It was the legend which caused John Higley some trouble. In the authoritative book, *Early Coins of America*, published in 1875, Sylvester Crosby tells us of the problem John Higley faced because the weight of his three pence coin did not come close to the comparable weight of an English coin.

"Being a frequent visitant at the public house, where at that time liquors were ... a common article of traffic, he was accustomed to pay his 'scot' in his own coin ... of the type which proclaims its own value to be equal to what was then the price of a potation — three pence."

His payment was rejected. Because John Higley wished to continue patronizing his local public house for refreshment, and because he did not wish to increase the cost of this type of recreation, some form of Yankee ingenuity was clearly required.

After a short interval, John Higley reappeared at the public house with a new form of payment. Its weight in fine copper and size were the same. There was, however, a difference in the engraving. On the obverse of the coin written around the same image of a deer is the legend: VALUE ME AS YOU PLEASE.

U-7-g (AE)
RX: Three Hammers

20

CHAPTER 9

We have no record confirming that his patronage then became acceptable, but it is a certainty as Sylvester Crosby has written of John Higley:

"... that should he be aware of the immense appreciation in the value of his coppers ... it would amply reward him for the insulting conduct of the publican."

U-7-g (AE)
OB: Higley
3 pence

"Millions for Defense"

*I*n 1785, Thomas Jefferson became the US Minister to France. He came to know the French well and witnessed the opening scenes of the French Revolution, which he believed had many of the same goals as the American Revolution. His main ambassadorial purpose was to secure economic support from America's primary European ally under the rule of the Bourbon King Louis XV.

F-1-c (AR)
Louis XV

Within the decade that followed, the French Revolution had taken place, and Jefferson returned to the US to serve as Secretary of State under George Washington. By 1796, there was a new minister to France — an aide de camp of Washington's named Charles Pinckney — who had urgent business to negotiate. The aggressive use of French sea power against the ships and crews of the new American republic had brought the two countries to the brink of war.

The French Foreign Minister Talleyrand was in the process of building his reputation as one of the monumental figures of European diplomacy. When Pinckney asked to start negotiations with Talleyrand's agents, (identified in the shorthand of history as X, Y, and Z), they replied that they would not even open negotiations unless a substantial bribe were paid. When John Adams succeeded Washington as President, he considered the XYZ affair so inflammatory that he kept it secret from Congress until the danger of war had passed. Pickney's actual reply to the extortion attempt was "No no — not a sixpence." Through legend and tradition, this quote has been memorialized as "Millions for defense — not one cent for tribute." And this is how the quote appears on a Hard Times Token struck about 40 years later.

U-8-b (AE)
Hard Times Token

The principles behind that sentiment were further proven to Talleyrand under the presidency of Thomas Jefferson. Jefferson had come to office in 1801 and, in that same year, learned that Spain, which had obtained the Louisiana Territory from France, was handing it back to France. Some presidents might have discerned no real difference in the effects on America of this diplomatic deal between two European powers. Jefferson did know the difference. While Spain was in decline, France not only represented dynamic new ideas, it was also in the early stages of its military expansion under Napoleon. The term Republique Francaise was striking terror throughout much of Europe, and Jefferson realized that under this new France, expansion to the American west would be effectively blocked.

There was already a symbol of change appearing in the Louisiana Territories. In 1767, the government of Louis XV had struck a sou for the French colonies featuring a crown over a wreath, and within the wreath three Fleurs de Lis (symbols of the House of Bourbon). These coins circulated unofficially in the Louisiana Territories, but one version of this coin would have given thoughtful Americans like Jefferson a special sense of what was happening in their backyard. Overstruck on top of the Fleur de Lis were the letters R.F. — Republique Francaise, now associated not just with its original ideas, but with war and military expansion.

U-7-gg (AE)
Sou

22

CHAPTER 10

Thomas Jefferson

Jefferson decided to act. In 1803, he secured $2 million from Congress for "extraordinary expenses" in the hope that this would at least secure from France the port of New Orleans and the guarantee of free navigation of the Mississippi. His timing could not have been better. Napoleon had already sent 35,000 troops to put down the rebellion of Toussaint l'Ouverture in Haiti and Santo Domingo, and was losing that colonial war to the rebels and to yellow fever. He could not hope to hold Louisiana without those bases and, at the same time, face the major conflicts with Britain which lay ahead. When Jefferson's commissioners made their proposal, the great Talleyrand no longer asked tribute from the Americans for the privilege of conferring with him. He made them a proposal which must have left them stunned. He would turn over all 800,000 square miles of the territories of Louisiana for $15 million. Jefferson, who had doubts as to his own power to exercise such a grand transaction, submitted this enormous bill for ratification by both the Senate and the House where it was overwhelmingly approved.

Talleyrand had not been able to exact tribute, but he was able to secure from Jefferson "millions for defense" and for the expansion of the new power in the western world.

A Fugitive From New Haven

Until the establishment of an official US currency by Congress in 1792, there was no central authorization to produce coins. The Americans dealt with this situation as well as they could. Ingenuity played a part; enterprise played a part; and chance played a part. A dead Indian, a Vermont legislator and an English officer all influenced the fate of early American coinage. One factory in Newburgh, New York, which produced coins for New York, Connecticut and Vermont, provides an example.

Abel Buel was the engineer for the New Haven Mint and a man highly regarded in his field. His grandson described "his genius as a mechanic ... and skill in invention." This New Haven mint produced Fugio cents of exactly the same Benjamin Franklin design as the Continental Dollar (Part 1, Chapter 7) and containing the Yankee advice: MIND YOUR BUSINESS. Before the United States Mint had its own mint, this penny was the first coin authorized for production by the United Sates Congress.

U-7-h (AE)
Fugio Cent

Abel Buel's son William was with him in the New Haven Mint and learned how to cut the dies for this and other coins from his talented father. William Buel required chemicals for the process of coin production and, on one occasion, was carrying to his home a jug marked Aqua Fortis. Enroute he found himself surrounded by a group of Indians who insisted that he was carrying a jug of rum which was to be made promptly available for their enjoyment. These unfortunate Indians — if they were seeking strong drink — found it indeed because Aqua Fortis was a brand name for nitric acid. One of the Indians died — and thereafter it was clear that William Buel could remain in New Haven only at the risk of his life.

He fled to one of the few other mints on this side of the Atlantic, Reuben Harmon's Mint House in Rupert, Vermont. Reuben Harmon had come from Suffield, Connecticut in 1768 and represented Rupert in the Vermont Legislature in 1780. This may have been helpful to him in securing the authorization to coin copper in June of

CHAPTER 11

army. Links from that chain are still on display at Trophy Point on the grounds of West Point. Machen's factory and the combined talent it represented produced well-known coins for three states including the Vermont plow coin referred to above, the New York Excelsior copper (Part 1, Chapter 8) and the Connecticut AUCTORI CONNEC copper.

U-7-z (AE)
*VT Copper
OB*

1785. Production took place in a building 16'x18' with rolling bars and also a furnace at one end to melt the copper — and at the other end stamping equipment. This small factory was able, with William Buel's participation, to strike as many as 60 coins per minute. One of the coins struck shows the sun rising behind Vermont's Green Mountains with a plow in the foreground and dated 1786. On the reverse is the legend: STELLA QUARTA DECIMA — 14th Star. Even though Vermont was not yet a state in 1786, the coin effectively represented the state's political objectives.

In April of 1787, an unusual co-partnership was signed between Reuben Harmon and the owners of Machin's Mills established that same year in Newburgh, New York as a "manufactory of hardware." The founder was Captain Thomas Machen (spelled with an e), an officer in the British army before the Revolution who joined the American army as an engineer during that war. Captain Machen was the army engineer responsible for building a chain of links across the Hudson River at West Point — a chain which prevented the British from passing through and dividing the continental

U-7-ccc (AE)
*Connecticut
Copper
OB*

Cartoon Tales

The concept of representing America's political parties in cartoons was originated during the 1860s by Thomas Nast, who also created the Republican elephant and Democratic donkey. These creatures were first put to work when Nast's cartoons portrayed the Tammany Hall political machine in New York City.

When Barry Goldwater was running against Lyndon Johnson for the presidency in 1964, he used the Republican elephant on imitation coins developed for his campaign in South Carolina. This state had traditionally been a southern bulwark of the Democratic party but, as the northern wing of that party became more liberal, the Goldwater strategists thought of a way to associate their state with the Republican elephant. They simply flooded the state with cheap copies of the 1694 Carolina token, featuring an elephant on the obverse, and on the reverse the words: GOD PRESERVE CAROLINA. Goldwater lost the election, but South Carolina remains today a bulwark of the southern Republican party.

The new American states had yielded the right to regulate and coin money exclusively to the Federal Government. This was one of the ultimate prerogatives of a sovereign state, and once the USA had established its own mint in 1792, there should have been no further need ever for private companies to issue emergency coinage. Andrew Jackson, the military hero who had driven the British out of New Orleans in the war of 1812, created that need during the second term of his presidency, 1833-1837. In those times, the young republic was coming into its own — expanding, investing and speculating. A privately owned but Federally sponsored company, the Bank of the United States, was used by the USA as its deposit bank and the Bank was lending out these funds to finance the American expansion. This Bank thought of itself as a Federal Reserve before that institution existed. When money became too plentiful, threatening inflation, the Bank of the United States would restrain its loans. Many businessmen resented this discipline and convinced President Jackson that the Bank was the enemy of free enterprise and should be shut down. When Jackson ran for reelection in 1832, he denounced the Bank as a monopoly and an enemy of American initiative. He was overwhelmingly reelected to a second term and proceeded to fulfill his campaign pledge. He ordered the Secretary of the Treasury to remove all government deposits from the Bank, effectively closing it down, and placed those funds in local (friendly) banks incorporated under state law. This was Jackson's "experiment" which he hoped would assure continued expansion with fiscal responsibility. The "experiment" failed.

With the fiscal restraints removed, there was a surge of speculation and a land boom. Many of the state banks had overextended themselves and, when the public sensed what was happening, there was a run on the banks — and the entire regional state banking system collapsed. Good coinage and money were horded as a defense against inflation and Hard Times Tokens were issued in copper by private entrepreneurs in the spirit of early

U-7-nn (AE)
OB: Elephant Token
RX: Legend

CHAPTER 12

Americans like Reuben Harmon. These first Hard Times Tokens were slashing cartoons on metal. One shows Jackson as a military man, sword in hand, while with the other hand he is grabbing a bag of money from the bank. It bears the legend: I TAKE THE RESPONSIBILITY. A second token shows Jackson on the obverse with the words: MY Experiment. MY Currency. MY Glory. My substitute for the US bank. The reverse portrays Jackson as a running boar over which is written: MY VICTORY. Underneath the boar we find the words: DOWN WITH THE BANK, and around the edge, the words: PERISH CREDIT, PERISH COMMERCE.

During Lyndon Johns's term in office, it was clear that the cost of silver was rising to a degree that would result in there being a greater value of silver in US coinage than the face value of the coins themselves. Bad money would drive out good, and silver coinage would simply be driven from circulation into the pockets of horders. Johnson, therefore, reissued all existing US silver coinage as clad pieces. These were skillfully made coins of base metal coated with silver (1965-1969). Johnson's efforts were noted by cartoonists all across the country, and a group of cartoons was assembled by "Coin World" for its issue of July 14, 1965 (next page).

U-8-g (AE)
Hard Times Token

U-8-e (AE)
Hard Times Token

COIN WORLD, Wednesday, July 14, 1965

Cartoonists View Debasement

For a period before this changeover was known by the public at large, it might have been possible for a very perceptive gambler to have made an assured killing at the Las Vegas casinos. Until shortly before the changeover to clad coins, Las Vegas used as its $1 chips the standard silver Morgan dollar, which was struck in tens of millions from 1878 to 1921. Our perceptive and fictional gambler might have presented his certified check for $10,000, received $10,000 worth of silver chips, and promptly left Las Vegas for his home town with his suitcase unopened. Three years later, *Yeoman's Guide Book of United States Coins* indicates that the value of most silver dollars in very fine quality would have appreciated from 200-300 percent. We have no record that this particular gamble was actually taken by anyone. Perhaps it was suspected that the management wouldn't have liked it.

U-6-u (AR)
Morgan Dollar

Part 2

COINAGE, CONFLICT— AND GOD

An American Debate

During the 1990s, there were lawsuits all over the United States over the issue of how religion relates to public school policy. For example:

- Are evangelical students at a public high school able to meet voluntarily with a high school teacher for prayer after school hours?

- Can the Ten Commandments be posted in public school classrooms?

These and other related issues may be in our courts for years.

The supporters of these proposals cite the First Amendment to the Constitution:

"Congress shall make no law ... abridging free speech ... or the right of people peaceably to assembly."

The opponents cite different parts of the very same First Amendment:

"Congress shall make no law respecting an establishment of religion."

To support the Jeffersonian concept of "separation of church and state," the Puritans were cited as an example of those original settlers who came to America in order to escape oppression by the established religion of England. Those who supported religious instruction in our public schools often acknowledged that early history, but said there was a difference between forbidding the establishment of religion in our schools and banning religion all together.

The American tradition, they said, was strongly supportive of religious belief. To support their position, the advocates show a continuing policy which "did not ban God." In 1864, influenced by the the Civil War, the Mint issued a two cent piece which appeared to associate religious belief in God with the future of the country. Directly over a U.S. shield bearing 13 stripes appear the words, "In God We Trust."

This same phrase was used up to our present times on the Benjamin Franklin half dollar which was struck from 1948 to 1963.

U-6-s (AR)
50 cents

In 1955, the 84th Congress passed Public Law #140 making the words, "In God We Trust," manditory on all US coins and currency. This was signed into law by President Eisenhower on July 11, 1955.

The opponents have their own coin experts. They were able to show that the coinage of New York, New Jersey, New Hampshire, Connecticut, Vermont and Massachusetts was consistently secular, both in its symbols and legends, one example being the one-cent copper issued by Massachusetts, which features a standing Indian.

U-6-d (AE)
Two cents

U-7-ee (AE)
One cent
Massachusetts

CHAPTER 1

Another representative coin was struck in New York in 1787 and featured the symbolic figure of Columbia, carrying the scales of justice. These two coins are typical of the many struck by the

U-7-q (AE)
"Immunis Columbia"

states, showing animals, birds, trees, plows and female patriotic figures like Columbia and Liberty. There is no hint on this early coinage of divine authority in the statehouse.

The general opinion is that only the Supreme Court will ultimately resolve this question. Some, however, believe that reviewing just 200 years of history on the relationship of religion to the state just scratches the surface. The complexities of this question go back for more than 2000 years.

Greek Gods on the Wing

The concept of divinity first appeared in nations around the Eastern Mediterranean basin, including Egypt. However, ancient Egypt did not produce coinage as a means of exchange, and the coinage produced later by the Ptolemies was really part of the Greek culture. Greece is where the story starts.

The role of the Greek gods fit easily into Greek society because these gods were very human. They lived, loved, hunted and played just as the mortals did. The gods had one special role, however, as protectors of a specific place, whether this was a spring or a river or a city-state. In the case of the Greek city-state, moreover, this was not an empire ruled by a divine, all-powerful leader but a republic which depended for its security on the support of its people and their worship of its protecting god or goddess. The rulers of the Greek city-state did not consider themselves divine, but they were able to use divine protection to mobilize their subjects toward their goals. When in 490 B.C. the Persian King Darius launched an assault on Athens, all of the Greek city-states were threatened. But the expected help from Greek allies did not arrive on time. At the city of Marathon, the Athenians met the more powerful Persians alone and secured the victory. The glory of Marathon was attributed by the Greek people not just to the leaders and citizens of Athens, but above all to the protection of the city's goddess Athena.

M-8-a (AV)
Daric
OB: Darius, King of Persia

G-1-c (AR)
Drachm
OB: Athena

The reverse of the Greek coin below features the famous owl of Athens. This owl, symbolizing wisdom and learning, also represented the spirit of the goddess Athena. The Greeks at Marathon had seen an owl flying over the battlefield and believed this was Athena in another form who had appeared in order to assure their victory. This was celebrated in Aristophones' play "The Birds" written in 414 B.C. in these lines:

"How we drove the ranks before us
Ere the close of eventide
As we closed an owl flew o'er us
And the gods were on our side."

G-1-c (AR)
Drachm
RX: owl

CHAPTER 2

Another flying divinity played a major role as a symbol of the power of the gods. In 420 B.C., an eagle head was struck on a Greek one-half stater to honor the Olympic games which originated on the island of Elis.

G-1-e (AR)
One-half Stater

The expression of the eagle is fierce and proud — and well it might be. This is no ordinary bird of prey but the eagle of Zeus and, therefore, symbol of the King of the pantheon of Greek gods. This coin was struck to celebrate the Olympic festival, and the only conflict associated with it is the conflict on the Olympic fields of sport — the annual games between former foes from all around the Greek world. That would change. The eagle of Zeus some 400 years later would be much involved in the mortal combat of those times.

Rome, The Republic and the Rise of the Caesars

We usually think of Rome as the great empire famous in history and literature as the ancient world's superpower. Rome was born, however, almost 500 years before its golden age when the city rose against its Etruscan king and declared a republic in 509 B.C. The birth of Rome is symbolized by the famous myth that her founders — twins Romulus and Remus — were raised and nursed by a wolf.

R-6-j (AR)
RX: wolf suckling Romulus and Remus

The city-state of Roma then formed a Latin league with neighboring cities in order to face the attacks of the Gauls. That alliance broke down. Rome was defeated by the Gauls, and was then occupied and ransomed. Nevertheless by the year 290 B.C., the Roman city-state was in control of most of Italy. This included the Greek cities of southern Italy where some of the finest mint facilities had been established.

As the Romans looked across the Mediterranean at their neighbors and potential enemies, they needed the blessing of the gods. Being an eminently practical people, they simply adopted the full panoply of gods from the Greeks. In 269 B.C., the Romans began production of silver coins featuring Zeus — now given the Roman name of Jupiter — and a helmeted war goddess representing ROMA clearly modeled on Athena. Among other borrowed divinities were the war god Mars (for the Greek Ares) and the goddess of Victory (for the Greek Nike). A didrachm of the third century B.C. shows Janus, the god of new beginnings, on the obverse.

R-6-c (AR)
Didrachm
OB: Janus

Roman coinage, like Greek coinage, was designed to seize the eye and to transmit a powerful message, which explains why the workmanship was generally so much better executed than the portraits on most coinage in the modern world.

That message was designed to transmit the pagan religion as a spiritual force designed to support the goals of the nation. The gods and goddesses, whether on Mount Olympus, hunting with Diana, or conducting war with Mars, were always in alliance with the rulers of the country. Jupiter had great moral force — but he had no battalions. Therefore, for the first 500 years of Rome's existence, it could be said that, just as in Greece, there was no conflict between faith and state.

CHAPTER 3

R-1-aa (AR)
Denarius
Julius Caesar

The last 80 years of the Roman republic, however, included political ruptures so severe that the state was submerged by conflict between dominant military personalities — Marius vs. Sulla, Julius Caesar vs. Pompey, and then Octavian vs. Marc Antony. As the competition for power within Rome increased, her military leaders started to issue their own coinage. Sulla issued his own coins, but at least kept the tradition of featuring no living ruler.

Julius Caesar ended that tradition with a series of coins featuring himself as ruler, and his early assassination failed to restore the old tradition. Brutus himself, as we've seen, finally struck his own portrait on his own coinage (see page 5). Marc Antony, a partner with Octavian in the coalition which defeated Brutus, also struck his own coinage when planning to set up his power base in Egypt (see page 6).

The concept of Roman leadership was undergoing a sea change. A coin was struck on Julius Caesar's behalf which some experts consider to be a coin of mourning because it shows a veiled head of Caesar. Others believed that Caesar was still very much alive because it has struck around the portrait the words "Dictator in Perpetuity." The ultimate change in direction had occurred in the Roman Senate which consecrated Julius Caesar as a divine person in 44 B.C. After Octavian finally defeated Marc Antony at the battle of Actium in 31. B.C., the nation was ready for unity and for peace. Octavian was the grandnephew of Julius Caesar and Caesar's will had named him his adopted son. This high-born heir had no competitors and acceded to power in 27 B.C. as Augustus Caesar, the first Emperor of Rome. Here was clearly the descendant of a divine person. The gods were about to be represented by a living man on the throne of the world's first power. The gods were also about to get their battalions.

The Descent of the Gods

The Roman Republic would never have been described as a pure democracy, but power was somewhat dispersed. Generals always had leverage and, in addition, there was an established power base. The old families of Rome formed the basis for the Patrician Party; the Equestrians represented the rising business class; and even the Plebians — the ordinary citizens — included individuals who were able to rise much above their original station.

These parties continued to influence Roman affairs after the Caesars came to power — especially the old Patrician families in the Senate which was occasionally consulted and sometimes listened to by the Emperor. However, there were to be no additional triumvirates ruling Rome. The empire had one man as Emperor and ruler. Because Julius Caesar had been declared divine, his adopted son, Augustus, and the future heirs to the throne, were also divine. Julius Caesar was clearly the inspiration for what followed.

It was important for the public to recognize that Augustus had not only acquired the authority but also the divinity which the senate had bestowed on his famous forebearer. This was important for the entire line of succeeding emperors and the claim of sanctification — DIVUS — now appeared on Roman coinage.

R-2-a (AE)
Dupondius
Augustus
"Holy Augustus Father"

R-5-o (AV)
Aureus
OB: Julius Caesar
RX: M Agrippa Desig
(see Appendix)

What mattered most, however, was that as other nations fell under the Roman sway, the empire absorbed people and culture from those subject nations, but insisted that they accept Roman concepts of religion. The religion itself was not that difficult to accept because there was no written doctrine, no dogma and no moral code. The only "sin" was failing to accept the rigid ritual, the sacrifices and, of course, the divinity of their ruler.

That ruler was also the commander in chief of the army — the imperator — and that army brought with it the Roman military ensigns featuring the eagle of Jupiter which accompanied the legions throughout the Roman domain. The diverse people under Roman control needed a divine force to unify them not just under the mythical gods, but under the manifest power of one living representative of those gods — the Emperor of Rome.

The legions of Rome were also accompanied by large statues of eagles carried by carefully selected eagle bearers (aquilifers) who were prepared to die protecting their charge — and sometimes did. What usually happened when the Roman faith confronted the faith of a subject people may be illustrated by the occupation of Britain. In the Summer of 43 A.D., four Roman legions landed in Kent under the command of a young, but experienced, veteran commander of previous campaigns named Vespasian. The Celtic inhabitants must have been staggered to see this highly disciplined army land

CHAPTER 4

from across the channel and then to see a small accompanying force (which included the Emperor Claudius) riding on elephants.

The arrival of the Roman gods, however, was less shocking because it happened over a period of decades. The Celtic inhabitants were able to observe the similarity of their gods to the Roman gods. The war god Mars, for example, was found to represent the same spirit as the important Celtic god Nodens, the cloud maker. The druid priests of Britain, however, had no way of fitting in with the new credo and, following the occupation, they simply disappeared from the scene.

During this same period, 2,000 miles across the empire in Judaea, quite a different story was developing. Pontius Pilate, the same Roman procurator who presided over the trial of Jesus, had ordered a troop of soldiers with their ensigns brought into the center of Jerusalem. It was Josephus, a former commander of the Judaean army, and then a historian at the Roman court, who has left this account of what happened on that occasion:

"Now Pilate who was sent as procurator into Judaea by Tiberius sent by night those images of Caesar that are called ensigns into Jerusalem. This excited a very great tumult among the Jews when it was day; for those that were near them were astonished at the sight of them as indications that their laws were trodden under foot; for those laws do not permit any sort of image to be brought into the city ... A vast number of people came running out of the country. These came zealously to Pilate to Caesarea and besought him to carry those ensigns out of Jerusalem and to preserve their ancient laws inviolable; but upon Pilate's denial of their request, they fell down prostrate on the ground and continued immovable in that posture for five days and as many nights.

On the next day Pilate sat upon his tribunal in the open market place and called to him the multitude as desirous to give them an answer; and then gave a signal to the soldiers that they should all by agreement at once encompass the Jews with their weapons; so the band of soldiers stood around about the Jews in three ranks ... Pilate also said to them that they should be cut to pieces unless they would admit of Caesar's images and gave intimation to the solders to draw their naked swords. Hereupon the Jews as it were at one signal fell down in vast numbers together and exposed their necks bare and cried out that they were sooner ready to be slain than that their law should be transgressed. Hereupon Pilate was greatly surprised at their prodigious superstition and gave order that the ensigns should be presently carried out of Jerusalem.

R-6-g (AR)
OB: Domitian
RX: Roman Ensigns

Clearly Judaea was a nation in turmoil not so much because it objected to the Romans as foreign rulers, but because the Roman gods and their ensigns violated the Second Commandment: "Thou shalt not make unto thee a graven image ... [nor] bow down unto them."

The graven images referred, of course, to idols, worshipped as divine creatures.

When Jesus of Nazareth arrived in Jerusalem at the end of his ministry, he encountered a group who considered him a heretic and believed they could prove him an opponent of the Roman tax laws requiring tribute by all Judaean subjects into the Roman treasury. To prove this in his own words, they asked Jesus whether it was lawful to pay tribute to Caesar and this was the reply (Mathew 22):

Show me the tribute money. And they brought him a penny.

And he sayeth unto them, whose is this image and subscription?

They say unto him, Caesar's.

Then sayeth he unto them, Render therefore unto Caesar the things which are Caesar's and to God the things which are God's.

With this diplomatic reply, Jesus turned away the implication that he favored a tax revolt against Rome. He chose not to confront the divine authority (described on the reverse of the coin as PONTIFEX MAXIM (the highest priest) but in due course, it was his followers who would confront and overcome the divinity of the Emperor and the gods.

Conflicts of nations over territory may be compromised, but a conflict between the many Roman gods and one supreme God cannot. An explosion in Judaea became inevitable. Starting in 66 A.D., the Jews started what has been called the First Revolt. It lasted for four years during which the rebels raised an army, protected Jerusalem's walls, inflicted real damage on the Roman occupiers, and issued their own coinage. No graven image, human or animal, appears on these coins.

In 68 A.D., the Romans designated a new commander of the Roman forces — Vespasian, now 25 years more experienced than when he had helped to subdue the Celts in Britain. His task was to finish this Judaean rebellion.

Josephus, long before he was a historian in Rome, had been a high-ranking priest and also a commander of the Judaean forces in Galilee. His military career ended suddenly when he and 12 other men were trapped in a cave by Vespasian's forces. The group debated whether to surrender, but held out until only Josephus and one other soldier remained. The two men then surrendered and Vespasian was on hand to inspect his high-ranking captive.

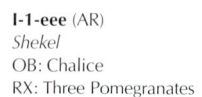

R-1-cc (AR)
Denarius
OB: Tiberias
RX: "Pontifex Maxim"

I-1-eee (AR)
Shekel
OB: Chalice
RX: Three Pomegranates

At that stage, there was every prospect that Josephus would be led as a prisoner through the streets of Rome — a human trophy as part of the victory parade. However, when Josephus faced his captor, he changed his own fate by the simple means of hailing Vespasian as the next Emperor of Rome. In those times foretelling the events of the future — auguring — was highly regarded in Roman society. In fact, Rome had a special college of priests (augures) which trained them to interpret signs. Did this commander of a strange people with their strange God have access to special powers of augury? Or did Josephus have some special knowledge of what was happening in the Roman capitol?

It was, in fact, true that the situation in Rome was deteriorating badly. Emperor Nero, who had started his reign well by delegating authority, lowering taxes and reforming the laws, ended his tenure as the playboy of the empire, spending and building wildly. After the great fire in Rome of 64 A.D. (which Nero blamed on the Christians), there were epidemics throughout the city and the people began to lose confidence in their leader. Nero's continuing raids on the treasury and open rebellion in both Gaul and Spain finally, in 68 A.D., resulted in the senate's condemnation of Nero to death. He is thought to have avoided that sentence by taking his own life. It was quite possible that Josephus had followed these events because, as a young man in his twenties, he had sailed to Rome to help fellow priests who had been imprisoned there. Poppaea, Nero's latest wife, helped him secure their release. Clearly he had good contacts in the capitol city.

R-2-ee (AE)
Nero fiddles

The year that followed, 69 A.D., was called the Year of the Four Emperors. There had not been such chaos since the last days of the republic. Otho succeeded to the throne and was then ousted by Vitellius, who was then in turn ousted by Vespasian. The commander had returned from Judaea to take the throne after delegating his military authority there to his son, Titus. Vespasian was able to secure his position firmly, starting the Flavian dynasty of emperors. Josephus, now a confirmed prophet, then took up his residence in the court to advise the Emperor of future events affecting imperial fortunes.

R-1-hhh (AR)
Denarius
OB: Otho

R-1-i (AR)
Denarius
OB: Vitellius

Judaea now faced the grimmest possible fate. By 70 A.D., Titus had occupied Jerusalem and burned the temple to the ground. The eagle on the ensigns of Titus' legions stood over the ruins of the center of monotheistic belief. Today one can still see the arch of Titus, commemorating this victory, quite near the coliseum in Rome where so many Christian and Jewish martyrs died for their faith. On the inside of this arch is a sculptured relief which shows the enormous, captured seven-branch menorah — the religious symbol of Judaea — being hauled through the streets of Rome during the victory parade.

From the Arch of Titus

The emperor Vespasian had his son's victory commemorated in a way that would serve as a visual reminder to all other provinces of Rome. He issued a large bronze showing his own portrait on the obverse, and on the reverse an armed Roman soldier guarding a mourning Jewess. Around this scene are scripted the words "Judaea Capta." As Isaiah had prophesied, "... she, being desolate, shall sit upon the ground."

R-4-b (AE)
Judea Capta
(see Glossary)

R-6-ddd (AR)
RX: Eagle

R-6-ddd (AR)
Cistophorus
OB: Vespasian

The Jews of Judea had been defeated, but the Jews of the Roman Empire were very much a part of the scene. At the time of the rebellion, they were already major participants in the life of cities from Alexandria in Egypt to Rome itself where they constituted ten percent of the one million population. Even those who had been taken to Rome as slaves could acquire freedom at a price. This was part of an old Roman tradition. There was in addition the biblical instruction that the Jewish community itself was obligated to pay for the redemption of their co-religionists from slavery.

The growing diaspora, however, kept its ties to Jerusalem. We see clear evidence of this in a case which was argued by Cicero, the great advocate of Julius Caesar's time. He defended Lucius Flaccus, a former governor of an eastern Roman province accused of confiscating the sums contributed by its Jewish residents, according to their annual tradition, for transfer to the temple in Jerusalem. The amount seized by Flaccus was 75,000 didrachms (two denari), the equivalent in value to 75 pounds of gold. Cicero won his case and the contribution remained in the Roman treasury. Toward the end of the first century, as we will see, the empire would determine a simpler and more direct way for such contributions to reach the federal treasury.

The Circumcision War

When the one great power of the ancient world, Rome, defeated its rebellious colony Judea in 70 A.D., that should have been the end of the story, but it was not.

The Roman emperors had difficulty forming a consistent policy of either conciliation or hostility towards their latest colony. In the 60 years following the destruction of the temple, the zigs and zags are reflected in Roman coinage of the time. These led to a second revolt.

The Emperor Domitian not only continued the tribute tax which had been in effect at the time of Jesus, but also determined that all Jews, wherever they lived in the empire, should pay the Roman treasury the Fiscus Judaicus, a two denarii tax which they had formerly paid to the now destroyed temple at Jerusalem — an insulting reminder of their defeat. This measure of Domitian's caused such a furor that his successor Nerva modified the decree and reverted to the traditional method which existed before the Jewish war. The tax itself was not entirely removed, but insult was not added to fiscal injury. In recognition of the modification, Nerva struck a Sestertius at left:

Left: **R-3-z** (AE)
OB: Nerva, 96-98 AD
RX: Palm Tree, (the Hebrew National symbol) with inscription CALUMNIA SUBLATA FISC. JUDAICI — "Removal of the insult of Jewish tax."

The Jews who remained in Judea following the Jewish war were concentrated in the area south of Jerusalem around the town of Hebron. Many of them were lease-holding peasants and, under the reign of Hadrian, they should have fared well. Hadrian's policies favored progressive development for all of the Roman provinces and that development included extensive public works and particularly favored the improvement of agriculture. The province of Judea was included in these programs and the Judean farmers would have benefited from them.

R-2-k (OR)
OB: Hadrian 130-131 AD
Head left
(See appendix)

CHAPTER 5

Hadrian was, in fact, confident enough of the Judeans' acceptance of Roman rule, that he planned a triumphful visit in the year 130 A.D. This visit was commemorated by a coin which is similar to those showing Hadrian's welcome in other parts of the realm.

R-2-k (OR)

RX: The emperor Hadrian is shown on the reverse of this coin being welcomed by a woman and three small children, holding palm leaves over an altar. The inscription around this image reads: ADVENTI AUG IUDAEAE — "Arrival Before the Jews."

Within two years of that visit, Judea was again in revolt. By the time the coin was circulated — five or six years later — Judea had again been crushed and even its name eliminated. Hence forth it would be referred to in the Roman Empire as Syria-Palaestina.

What was it that sparked this second revolt of the Jews?

For the rulers of the super power sitting in Rome the causes must have been murky. They were overseeing a realm which stretched from Hadrian's Wall in Britain to the Arabian Desert, with all of the inhabitants free to enjoy the Pax Romana. Roman roads, harbors and gymnasia reached out into the most distant provinces, but there was one other feature of Roman rule which had no physical form but which was equally pervasive. The inhabitants were expected to adopt the prevailing Graeco Roman culture, which included reverence for the emperor and enforcement of royal decrees throughout the empire. The assimilated Jews living in cities throughout the realm, including those in Rome, adjusted to the Roman culture, while keeping their faith and identity. It must, of course, have disturbed them when Hadrian during his visit to Judea, established a Roman colony, Aelia Capitolina, on the former site of the Jerusalem temple. This did not, however, directly impose upon their daily way of life, nor on the practice of their faith. The temple itself had been gone for over a half a century. Hadrian did, however, make one decision which would effect the basic practice of the faith of every Jewish family in the empire. He had amended the earlier decree of Domitian, which forbade castration throughout the empire, so that it also included a ban on circumcision. The ban was to be enforced upon pain of death. Hadrian may not even have been fully aware that he was targeting a religious covenant — a right as basic to Judaism as Baptism is to Christianity.

The assimilated Jews of Rome and other cities may have felt that there were ways to subvert this law. But to the simple and traditional peasant communities of Judea, there were only two choices: to give up their faith, or to resist by force of arms. Within an area of about 300-400 square miles south of Jerusalem and centered around Hebron, the Judean peasants organized, collected taxes and dues, formed an army and selected a leader. That leader was Simon Bar Kochba, who was able to lead a guerilla war against the Roman legions for more than three years.

As coinage was the principal means of propaganda at that time, it was part of Bar Kochba's campaign to show that the ruler of Judea was no longer the Emperor Hadrian. A new Hebrew coinage had to be minted within the territory he controlled. The Jews could no longer produce their own metal flans for original coinage as they had during the Jewish war. Therefore, in order to create their own coinage, it was necessary first to have a very large inventory of Roman coinage. It was necessary to organize within their small territory a program of tax collection, contributions and raids on Roman outposts so that a large supply of the imperial coinage would be available in both silver and bronze. The rebels then established a mint to overstrike these coins with their own images designed to stir up Jewish national feeling, overstriking the widely-circulated Roman denarius with Hebrew images — thus converting them into quarter shekels, to recognize their own leadership and to recall the temple.

I-2-w (AR)
¼ *Shekel*
OB: Simon within a wreath
RX: Urn and palm branch with inscription: "Freedom of Jerusalem"
132-135 A.D.
(see Appendix)

I-2-p (AR)
OB: Temple with scrolls
RX "For the freedom of Jerusalem"
132-135 A.D.
(see Appendix)

Hadrian's Aelia Capitolina colony was designed to "eclipse the God of the Jews," and the decree on circumcision was designed to change their religious practice. He had the military means to achieve these goals, and the rebels of Judea lost the battle, striking their last coins in 134 A.D.

However, they won their war objectives. Hadrian died in 138 A.D., having that same year adopted Antonius Pius as his heir — an emperor who ruled Rome for the next 22 years, and who wanted peace throughout the empire. One of the earliest decrees of his regime amended Hadrian's law and authorized the rite of circumcision "for the sons of the Jews alone." The way of life and faith of Jews throughout the empire was therefore preserved by the peasants of the Judean plains.

The section of the Temple shown on this coin was one point of reference for a miniature reconstruction of the Temple and the ancient city of Jerusalem. It is located on the grounds of the Holy Land Hotel in the capital of modern Israel.

The Circumcision War is one of those rare examples of faith-state conflict in which the state tries to impede or eliminate a religious practice. One of the coins struck by Bar Kochba, however, illustrates an opposite situation in which the faith and state are one, and are in fact the same people. According to the bible, the first monotheistic place of worship was the tabernacle or tent of meeting built by the Israelites during their sojourn in Sinai under the leadership of Moses. The high priests of that tabernacle were the two sons of Aaron. According to the Book of Numbers, Chapter 10, these were the Lord's instructions to Moses:

> *"Make thee two trumpets of silver ... and they shall be unto thee for calling of the congregation ... at the door of the tent of meeting ... And when ye go to war in your land against the adversary ... then ye shall sound the alarm with the trumpets."*

Aaron's sons, therefore, could summon the people to worship (a function of faith) or to war (a function of the state).

Bar Kochba overstruck the symbol of the two trumpets onto a Roman Denarius as a memorial to events which had occurred 1300 years earlier.

I-x-x (AR)
¼ Shekel
Trumpets of Aaron's sons
(Coin enclasped)

Scene painted by author representing the sons of Aaron and the tent of meeting (Book of Numbers, Chapter 10).

The Death March of the Gods on the Road to Constantinople

The footsteps of the ancient Roman Empire have left tread marks across Europe and around the Mediterranean. Travelers still wonder at the Roman pool at Bath, England — built over natural hot water mineral springs with nearby bathhouses and changing rooms. These rooms were heated by "modern" plumbing — hot water pipes running directly from the natural springs.

Another wonder of engineering, architecture and imagination is the Pont de Gard — the many-arched aqueduct in Nimes, France. These two examples represent the range and durability of Rome's mark on history.

But where are the gods? How could a system of belief which permeated the Greco Roman world have disappeared so completely? The gods are, of course, still with us in some ways. We observe Venus and Mars still circling above us in the heavens. Apollo and Jupiter still pervade our literature. Even in commerce, we can find images of Neptune on the doors of some seafood restaurants. The gods have not disappeared from our culture — just from our prayers.

Pont de Gard

Gibbon, in his book *The Decline and Fall of the Roman Empire,* attributed Rome's demise to the "triumph of barbarianism and religion." The religion which triumphed, therefore, could not have been the faith of the Roman gods. In fact, that faith and the empire it served remained at the zenith of its power for only about two centuries after the time of Hadrian. It was during those two

CHAPTER 6

centuries that the forces to which Gibbon referred worked together — barbarians from without and religion from within — to demolish the western Roman nation state. Imperial power had brought captives, traders and slaves from foreign lands, often bringing with them different codes of belief. Isis, the Egyptian god of motherhood, became widely accepted as did Mithras, the Parthian Sun God. Most important of all was the God of the Christians who not only preached a doctrine of peace for which Rome was now hungry but also preached hope in the afterlife for the poor and the downtrodden. At the end of the second century, some of Rome's most educated men were losing their faith in the Greco Roman Pantheon. A tombstone of the time read "I believe in nothing beyond the grave." This weakening faith also bred a reaction from the Roman traditional believers who feared that Christianity might fill the vacuum and who therefore attacked it. The author Celsius wrote in the *True Word*:

> "It is only the simpletons, the ignoble, the senseless — slaves, women and children — whom Christians can persuade — wool dressers and cobblers ... the most common men."

With the passing generations, the descendants of Rome's captives and slaves, so many of whom had been killed by wild animals in the coliseums, became free Roman citizens. No doubt many of these descendants kept the monotheistic faith for which their forbearers had died. During the third and fourth centuries, as the barbarian forces increased their military pressure on Rome's borders, there were millions of Romans who did not share the established faith. The early church and the state were therefore in conflict. How would a divided Rome meet the barbarian assaults?

The emperor Diocletian who ascended to the throne in 284 A.D. took action to reform and reorganize the empire.

R-6-I (AE)
Follis
Diocletian

To meet the growing military threat from the north and east, he felt there should be an eastern emperor as well as a western one. He also felt that he could not have his capital south of the Alps. He moved it therefore from Rome to Nicomedia just south of Byzantium. The seed of the future Byzantine Empire had been planted. The Roman Empire was no longer ruled from Rome.

The division of Roman power, however led inevitably to jealousy and conflict. Diocletian's autocratic system broke down following his reign. It became the destiny of one future ruler to restore order, to change the faith of the Mediterranean world, and to save Rome by transforming it and by transplanting it.

The Emperor Constantine came to power in 307 A.D. and five years later found himself in an armed struggle for control of the empire against Maxentius, his rival under the Diocletian system, and who was the candidate of Rome's Praetorian Guard. The two imperial forces met at Saxa Rubra just north of Rome.

The composition of these two armies was influenced by the forces affecting all of Roman society at that time. Because there had been few conquests, there were fewer slaves. Moreover, the Romans had been limiting the size of their families and since the time of Hadrian the population had been in decline. Roman law recognized the *penuria hominum* — the manpower shortage — which was having a major effect on the composition of the military forces.

The soldiers under Maxentius were generally pagan but foreign influence was evident in the high percentage of those who believed in the foreign Parthian sun god, Mithras. This eastern god was unlikely to inspire the same loyalty in Maxentius' Roman army as the ancient eagles of Jupiter would have done. In Constantine's army moreover there was a new and untraditional element — a very large number of Christians. How would they fight for an empire which had been suppressing their religion?

Constantine resolved that question. Shortly before the battle started, he dreamed he was told to mark his soldiers' shields with the Chi-Rho monogram — the sign of Christ. After he did this, his troops proceeded to throw Maxentius's forces into the Tiber River.

R-6-m (AE)
Follis
Constantine

Constantine himself had been exposed to the relatively new faith because his own mother was a Christian. We cannot know whether the events of this critical battle represent a genuine change of the Emperor's faith or a brilliant move of psychological warfare. We do know that when Constantine and his troops entered Rome, it was clear that he had become the single master of the Roman Empire.

The next eighteen years changed the history of the world. The following year, 313 A.D., Constantine issued the Edict of Milan extending toleration to all faiths. He greatly increased the size of his army to assure that he would be in control of both the eastern and western parts of the empire. Whatever his true religion may have been at the time of his battle for the throne, in 323 A.D. Constantine made the irrevocable decision to declare himself a Christian. Thereafter, no more gods or goddesses appeared on Roman coinage. Two years following his personal conversion, the emperor summoned a convocation of all Christian bishops to the Counsel Constantine at Nicaea near his capital at Nicomedea. The purpose of the Council was to resolve the many conflicts which had developed in the young religion so that Christianity could replace the very sick pagan faith to represent the religious expression of the Roman empire itself.

There was just one final step which this remarkable leader would take in order to insure that a reinvigorated Roman Empire would survive the dangers it was still facing. In the Year 330 A.D., Constantine turned his back on both Nicomedia and Rome to establish a new city in Byzantium which he called Nova Roma, but which in fact soon assumed the name of its great founder as Constantinople.

Constantine surely knew he had accomplished much in establishing this new capital — but he cannot possibly have imagined the enormous import of his achievement.

The Western Empire, as represented by Rome, had only another 150 years to live. Its pagan faith would die with it. Constantine had transplanted this civilization to a new soil where it would blossom as a new Byzantine state fueled by a militant Christianity and strategically placed to resist the Moslem faith rising in the east. It would also become the center of the new Greek Orthodox form of Christianity, the first major schism within the church and one which would change the form of worship not just of Greece, but of eastern Europe and Russia.

Nova Roma would outlast classical Rome by almost 1000 years. The original western empire meanwhile was being subjected to growing pressure. As the Huns moved west from China, driving the eastern Goths before them, both groups put increasing stress all along the borders of Rome's northern provinces. In 367 A.D., Rome had to withdraw its forces from Britain to reinforce its defenses.

The Roman response to the Barbarian incursions was not always military. The western barbarian tribe, the Visigoths, had not only accepted a more settled way of life, but even played a part in the politics and defense of the empire. Alaric, King of the Visigoths, was declared a Roman officer but that did not prevent him from sacking Rome in 410 A.D. He then seized the 16 year-old half sister of the Emperor Honorius named Galla Placidia and held her as hostage. The Visigoths, however, did not realize the treasure they had seized. In 414 A.D., following Alaric's death, she married his successor as King of the Visigoths, Ataulf, and reestablished good relations between the two peoples as Queen of the Visigoths. When her half brother Honorius died, her very young son succeeded as Emperor and Galla Placidia, as regent for her son, became the ruler of all of western Europe.

R-8-a (AV)
Solidus
Honorius

During the next century, the many German tribes secured control of most of the empire except Italy. In addition, Britain was now controlled by the Saxons and the Vandals had taken over Spain and North African Carthage. While the Western Empire sank, the Eastern Empire at Constantinople had become strong enough in 468 A.D. under Leo I to raise a rescue force of 100,000 men hoping to salvage the west's North African territories. That effort failed — and with it Rome's last chance to survive. By 476 A.D., German troops made up the bulk of the Roman army defending the old capital. When these troops revolted, the last Roman emperor, the young Romulus Augustus, was sent into exile, and Odoacer, a German commander, took over the remains of the western Roman Empire.

R-8-bbb (AV)
Solidus
Leo I

Just 12 years later in 488 A.D., the eastern emperor Zeno, in Constantinople, arranged with an Ostrogoth leader, Theodoric, to lead his people into Italy in order to overthrow Odoacer. In this successful effort, he was able to bring Italy back into the Christian world.

R-8-c (AV)
Solidus
Zeno

The coins of Zeno still show on their reverse the remnants of paganism. They feature Victory, the former goddess, but now she is shown "aiding the cross."

By this time, the great power in the west was no longer an emperor but the Roman Catholic Pope. The Roman Popes were by no means satisfied with the religious practices of the Byzantine Christians who tended to compromise so as to find common ground with their subjects. In 517 A.D., papal legates arrived in Constantinople to insist that Anastasius enforce Catholic doctrine strictly. Anastasius replied to the Pope, "You may thwart me, Reverend Sir; you may insult me; but you may not command me." This was the early phase of the growing division within the Christian religion — ultimately resulting in the scchism between the Roman Catholic and Greek Orthodox churches.

R-8-d (AV)
Solidus
Anastasius

The eastern emperor Justinian was still considered a Roman emperor (537-582 A.D.), speaking better Latin than Greek, recodifying Roman law, and extending his rule over both eastern and western empires — including north Africa. He may have instituted the concept of the "divine right of kings," specifying that no one could be considered a valid ruler until crowned in the magnificent church he had constructed in Constantinople (still standing in today's Istanbul) — the Hagia Sophia. The faith and state were indeed one.

R-8-f (AV)
Solidus
Justinian

The quality standard of the gold solidi had been set for Byzantium, a standard which would be as stable as the eastern empire itself. As described in the writings of Cosmas Indico-Pleustes at that time "The gold money of the Roman Empire is accepted everywhere from end to end of the earth ... no kingdom has a currency to compare with it."

Within a generation of Justinian's death in 582, it became clear that the union of east and west could not last. The time had come for a separate, powerful and enduring Byzantine empire.

The Throne of Jesus

When we think of the Byzantine Empire and its culture today, we also think of icons — images or portraits of Jesus or his family members which are worshipped. These icons were not always associated with Byzantium. To the contrary, the first dynastic families who ruled the world's first Christian state were strongly opposed to them.

The story of this conflict of images is told in the Byzantine coinage of the times — coinage of a court so opposed to change of any sort that the weight of its gold coinage, the flat, unsculpted nature of its portraits, and the full-faced poses of the royal family members did not change from one century to the next for eight centuries.

There was, however, one major change, which was reflected in the coinage of the first four dynasties ruling Byzantium — a period of time running from 610 to 857 A.D. It was a struggle at court between a group identified as the iconoclasts, who believed in representing Christianity on the coinage by the simple representation of the cross, and their opponents, the image symbolists, who wished to create icons — that is images of Jesus and his family on Byzantine coinage.

Because the power to strike coins represented the power to project ideas we can see the philosophy of each dynasty reflected in the coinage of its time. The first three Byzantine dynasties were all iconoclasts, but at the end of two of these dynasties — the Heraclids and the Isaurians — the final rulers of these families were rebels, who supported image symbolism. In the long run, as the chart below illustrates, it was the Basilid Dynasty which settled the matter.

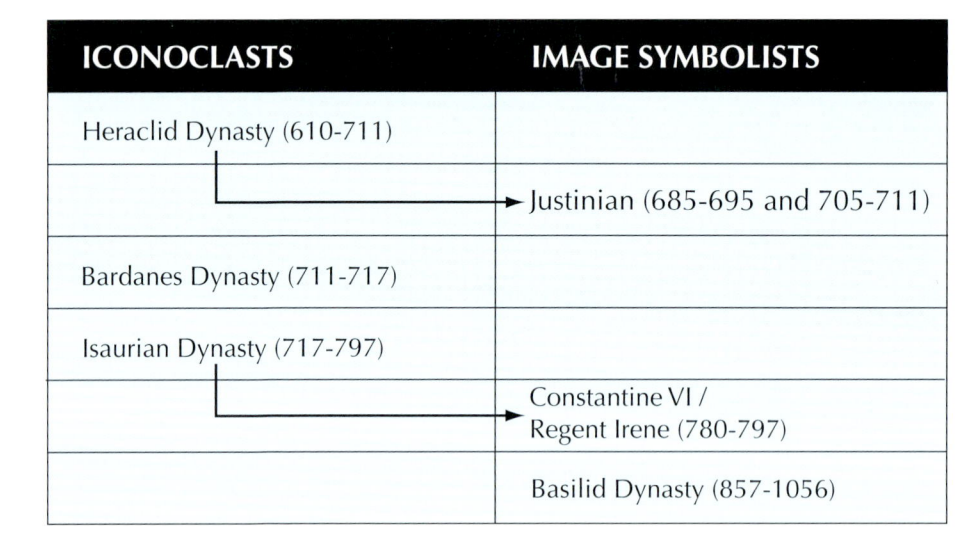

ICONOCLASTS	IMAGE SYMBOLISTS
Heraclid Dynasty (610-711)	
	Justinian (685-695 and 705-711)
Bardanes Dynasty (711-717)	
Isaurian Dynasty (717-797)	
	Constantine VI / Regent Irene (780-797)
	Basilid Dynasty (857-1056)

Heraclius, the first emperor of the new Byzantium, started his rule as the defender of his throne in a long and exhausting war with the Persians. It was a war that he won.

The state, however, remained in jeopardy because of the militant Moslem faith now spreading throughout the Arab world during the 7th Century. In 677 A.D., and again in 717 A.D., the Arabs were able to launch naval assaults against Constantinople. The eastern capital was able to withstand them, effectively confirming the judgement of Diocletian and Constantine that Rome had to be protected on its eastern frontier. Constantinople was, in fact, defended successfully for the next 700 years.

The dynasty of the Armenian Heraclid family represented the union of church and state on its coinage, featuring members of the royal family on the obverse of their gold solidi, and on the reverse a simple "cross potent" standing on a three or four-step pedestal. This cross was no longer accompanied by the pagan goddess of victory.

CHAPTER 7

R-8-i (AV)
Solidus
Heraclius and his son

It was, however, the last member of the Heraclid Dynasty, Justinian II, coming to power in 685 A.D., who made the greatest change in Byzantine coinage. Justinian II did not have an ordinary reign. He made a favorable peace with his Saracen, Moslem enemies, specifying that the Saracens were to send the empire tribute each year. Then he declared war on them again because the Saracen leaders paid the tribute in Arab Dinars instead of Solidi. Justinian was defeated and then overthrown by one of his own rebel generals, Leontius. That general spared his life but wanted to send a message that Justinian II was not the perfect leader (perfection being a requirement for the rulers of this theocratic empire). He ordered Justinian's nose to be split and thereafter Justinian II, dethroned in 695, carried the nickname "Rhinometus."

The turmoil of this emperor's reign was matched by a revolutionary change in the nation's coinage: a bust of Jesus was struck on the obverse of the gold Solidus bearing the legend SERVUS CHRISTI. It was probably not a coincidence that these coins featuring Jesus were struck at a time when the first Islamic coins were being struck by the Arabs. We can only surmise the turmoil this must have caused at court, which had vigorously opposed placing the family of Jesus on the coinage up to that point, but it did not keep Justinian II from returning to the throne in 705 A.D. and ruling for another six years.

R-8-zz (AV)
Solidus
OB: Jesus

By the year 717 A.D., the Moslem threat became critical when the Grand Vizier Suleiman sent a fleet to secure the straights above the Gold Horn near Constantinople. Using its secret weapon "Greek fire" — a mysterious flammable which was very difficult to extinguish by water, the Byzantine fleet mingled with the Saracen ships, setting many of them ablaze. By the end of August 718 A.D., virtually the entire Saracen fleet of 1800 vessels had been destroyed. The city of Constantinople was safe and the emperor guiding its victory, Leo III, was not only a military hero, but the founder of a new dynastic family — the Isaurians.

This new dynasty banned "sacred images," favoring instead the iconoclast philosophy of the Heraclids. There were to be no human icons. The bust of Jesus did not appear on Byzantine coins during this family's 80-year reign and the cross potent was restored. This reform, however, died with the Isaurians — Constantine VI, the last of that dynasty, was born in 771 A.D., coming to the throne at the age of 10 upon the death of his father. This all led his scheming mother, Irene, to assume the role of Regent, and in that role she engaged in both war and diplomacy — even negotiating the engagement of her son to the daughter of the western emperor Charlemagne.

Irene, who was Greek, was also a secret supporter of the sacred images and very carefully hoped to change the policy as it applied to Byzantine coinage.

As Constantine VI reached manhood, he demanded his full royal powers and for a while he secured them. Though he had at first subjected his mother to palace arrest, he shortly released her and then went off to fight the traditional Byzantine foes — the Saracens. He returned from the front to visit his wife, Theodote, who had just had a miscarriage. Using this opportunity, Irene induced a group of his supporters to seize her son and transport him to a section of the royal palace, the Porphyra, the very place where he had been born. His eyes were then cut out on the instructions of his mother. Irene, now the sole ruler was considered Orthodox in her faith, building convents, doing charitable works, and given the title "Most Pious Empress."

Charlemagne, the undisputed ruler of the west, hoped for the union of the two Roman Empires. Though the marriage of their children had never taken place, Charlemagne entered into negotiations to marry Irene herself. This effort also failed because of her failing health. The marriage that did not happen was a significant event because it marked the final separation of the east and west. When Charlemagne was crowned emperor of the west on Christmas day 800 A.D., the ceremony was performed at St. Peter's in Rome by Pope Leo III, who was thereafter under the Emporor's protection. Constantinople would no longer speak for Rome. Surprisingly, Irene issued no coins featuring the sacred images, perhaps because of the army's opposition, but the Isaurian ban was over. The images in due course would blossom.

The next great dynasty to rule Byzantium were the Basilids, members of the Armenian nobility who came to power in 857 A.D., and retained the throne for just under 200 years. Contrary to their predecessors, this dynasty favored the sacred images which became the best test and standard of their Orthodox faith.

R-8-op (AV)
Solidus
This Solidus of Romanus I shows Jesus enthroned.

Mary was also shown and is portrayed as the Mother of God, placing the crown on the head of Romanus III.

R-8-r (AV)
Solidus
Romanus III crowned by the Virgin Mary

The sacred images would remain on the coinage until the end of the Byzantine era. That came in 1453 by which time two major monotheistic religions encircled the Mediterranean — the Christians to the north (with the exception of southern Spain) and the Moslems to the south and east. Within a period of 40 years during the 15th century, the borders between the two faiths became relatively fixed. In 1448, the last Byzantine emperor, Constantine XI, came to the throne during the reign of the friendly Turkish Sultan Murad II. When Murad died in 1451, he was succeeded by his son, Mohammed II, whose aim was to make Constantinople his capital. The final drama was played out on May 29, 1453. Facing an overwhelming assault, Constantine gathered his followers around him, asked forgiveness of his sins, and then rode off with his best troops to fill a breach in the walls of Constantinople. Waves of enemy sabermen filled the breach, overwhelmed the defenders and then wandered through the empty streets of Constantinople looking for defenders. There were none left. The Turks found the remains of the last heroic emperor under the bodies of his troops and cut off his head. The coin struck by Mohammed II in 1453 featured no image whatsoever — in accordance with Moslem religious doctrine.

M-X-x (AR)
Silver Akche
Mohammed II, 1451-81

Thirty-nine years later, a balancing drama was played out. The Spanish royal houses of Castile and Aragon had been united by the marriage of Ferdinand and Isabella, who considered it their holy mission to rid Spain of all non-Christian influence. In the year 1492, the last Moslem outpost in Spain, at the magnificent fortress of Granada, was secured by the Catholic forces. The Moslem toehold in western Europe was eliminated.

By the last half of the 15th century, the long-term boundaries of Christianity had simply moved west — giving up Constantinople on its eastern front and gaining all of southern Spain on its western front. Ferdinand and Isabella made two other decisions in 1492 which had a long-term impact on world history: they expelled the 200,000 Jews of Spain who would not convert; and they dispatched Columbus to discover the western route to "India."

M-3-a (AV)
Double Excellente
RX: Combined Crests of Castile and Aragon

M-3-a (AV)
Double Excellente
OB: Ferdinand and Isabella

Defender of the Faith

*I*n the reign of Edward the Confessor, King of England in the year 1064, a rising young nobleman of his court, named Harold, on an inspection tour on an English ship, was blown by a storm onto the French coast of Normandy. This was an ill wind indeed, because William, the Duke of Normandy, had a longstanding claim on the English throne, having married a woman related to the Saxon royal family. William now had within his grasp a possible future occupant of that throne.

Winston Churchill in his book, *The Island Race*, notes: "It is probable that Harold swore a solemn oath to William to renounce all rights ... upon the English crown, and it is likely that if he had not done so, he might never have seen either crown nor England again."

So began a famous hostage case which had great consequences because the hostage was released.

When King Edward lay dying two years later, he named his young counselor, Harold, as his successor. The Saxon Council confirmed that choice and Harold was crowned King at Westminster Abbey. In the comfort and safety of his own people, Harold had forgotten his pledge to William. A pledge between the nobles in the feudal age, however, was not to be forgotten. The Norman invasion of England became inevitable.

William, having released his royal hostage, now had to transport his formidable Norman cavalry across the English Channel to collect his due. It is estimated today that perhaps 5,000 or 6,000 mail-clad, Norman knights and a few thousand archers — all mounted horsemen — confronted an equal number of Harold's foot soldiers, his ax and spear men. The Norman cavalry won the battle at Hastings, illustrated by the hand interpretation (below) of the Bayeux Tapestry.

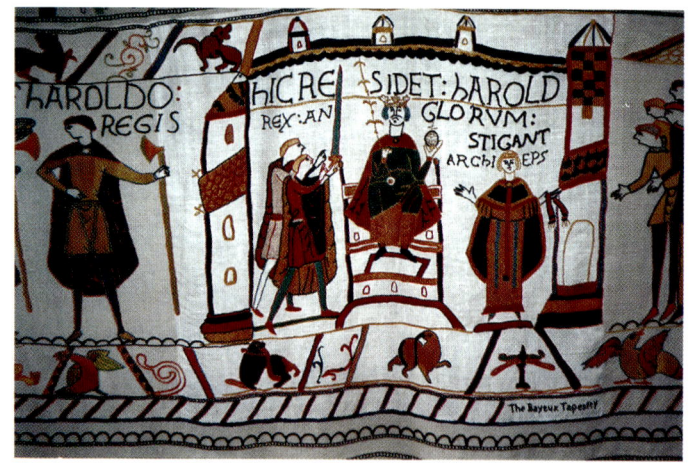

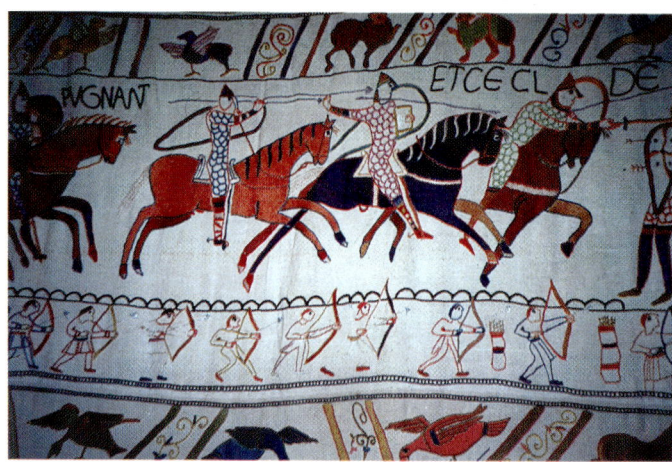

Two photos of interpretation of the Bayeux Tapestry courtesy of Mr. & Mrs. Michael Charnaud

CHAPTER 8

Harold died in that battle, and William the Conqueror was crowned King of England on the following Christmas. Because of William's vast holdings in France, England, unlike its Scandinavian neighbors, would from this point on be involved deeply in the affairs of the continent. This new King, however, did not want any continental power — including the church — to be too much involved in England. He moved against the papacy early in his reign. With his friend Lefranc as Archbishop of Canterbury, it was arranged that all abbots and bishops in England would be obligated to the King, quite apart from their church duties.

B-3-m (AR)
Penny
William the Conqueror

Relations with the church were to be decided by William who specified that his churchmen would recognize no Pope until he had approved. All correspondence between the Pope and the English church would be subject to royal censorship. Here was the first of the struggles between church and state which would continue in England for a period of more than 600 years.

During the reign of William's grandson, Henry II, in 1164, the King proposed a reform of church law under the Constitution of Clarendon, which would have ended the independence of the ecclesiastic courts from royal authority, and also would have ended the right to a final appeal to the Pope. This program was opposed by the Archbishop of Canterbury, the famous Thomas Becket, who fled to the continent to secure the Pope's help. Years later he returned home to a rousing welcome. Henry, in full court, surrounded by his closest advisors, declaimed: "What a pack of fools ... I have nourished ... that not one of them will avenge me of this upstart clerk." On December 29, 1170, the King was avenged. Four of his knights found Thomas Becket at the Canterbury Cathedral and there, in his own church, ended his life — but not his cause. The Clarendon Constitution did not go into effect.

Henry II's son Richard came to the throne in 1189 and was far more interested in foreign adventure and conquests than in affairs at home in Britain. He joined the King of France as a joint leader of the Third Crusade, but Richard — "the Lionhearted" — accrued the lion's share of the glory.

B-3-a (AR)
Penny
Richard the Lionhearted

In this role he was cooperating with the Pope's call to rescue Jerusalem from the Moslem rule of the Egyptian Saladin, while providing his nobles with glory and loot. A skilled general, he was able to capture both Acre and Jaffa in the Holy Land in 1191 and 1192, and from a high peak in the area, could secure a distant view of Jerusalem. That was as close as the crusaders got. Richard was called home to deal with problems in England, was kidnapped en route by the Duke of Austria, and finally ransomed in 1194 for 150,000 marks — twice the annual revenue of the English crown. King Richard was then recrowned in London, as a great feudal hero, but the third crusade ultimately failed to achieve its main goal, the liberation of Jerusalem.

England, however, had continuing problems much closer to home with its French Norman domains, which England continued to occupy and which represented about one-third of France. For about 300 years, the English forces did very well. Vast sections of French land remained under the English crown, some by inheritance, some by conquest, and some by marriage. Famous English heroes of history and literature participated in building this Anglo Gallic nation. Edward, the Black Prince, who lived in the middle of the 14th Century, was the popular ruler of Acquitaine in southwest France after it was seized by his father, King Edward III.

B-3-k (AR)
Demigros
Edward the Black Prince

Centuries of conflict in France had stirred up English opposition to all foreign influence, including the papal agents who were seen to represent an external institution. That perception became even stronger when the seat of the papacy moved in 1309 from Rome to Avignon in southern France. The Holy See remained there, subject to the French king, for the next seventy years. All of the Avignon Popes were French and, to the English, they ruled from an enemy land.

In 1369, an Oxford scholar named Wyclif proposed reducing the church's earthly powers in order to purify its spiritual ones. His proposal failed, but he then took a step which ultimately had much greater impact. With the help of his students, he translated the Bible into English so that the masses would be able to understand it.

While religion was becoming more widespread and more nationalistic, the church was being assaulted by a new foe — the bubonic plague — the Black Death, which greatly reduced the number of the clergy. According to *The Fourteenth Century, 1307-1399* by McKisack:

"By 1399 ... the ecclesiastic authority and the whole medieval ecclesiastic system [in England] had been openly and strenuously challenged."

The English crown meanwhile continued its claims and efforts to secure more French territory. Many English-speaking school boys learn from Shakespeare's *Henry V* of that King's famous victory at Agincourt in 1415. And they may also recall that he claimed, as a spoil of war, the hand of the French Princess Catherine. Henry arranged to be alone with her after the victory and Shakespeare records this dialogue (including the Princess's French accent):

Catherine: *"Is it possible dat I should love de enemi of France?"*

Henry: *"No ... For I love France so well that I will not part with a village of it."*

B-3-f (AR)
Gross
Henry V

England would soon give up much more than a village. Henry V could not have predicted the development of the world's best artillery by the French, and he could not have predicted the Maid of Orleans, Joan of Arc. This inspired peasant girl led a small convoy and rallied the French forces in 1430 so that the English, within twenty-five years after Agincourt, had to leave all of France except for the Port of Calais. Henry's and Catherine's son, Henry VI, struck a symbolic Anglo Gallic coin bearing his name. It was one of the last.

B-3-l (AR)
Grand Blanc
Henry VI

The decisive phase of the struggle between the church and the English state started about one century later. Henry VIII of the Tudor dynasty came to the throne in 1509, following the death of his older brother, Prince Arthur. Arthur's widow was Princess Catherine of Aragon, the daughter of Ferdinand and Isabella, and Henry promptly married her. This secured for him both a possible mother for his future heirs and a continuing link to the powerful Spanish royal house. Catherine was at Henry's side for the first 22 years of his reign. During the early years, Henry was militarily allied to the papacy and also to their Catholic majesties, Ferdinand and Isabella.

Before his brother's death, Henry had been trained to enter the church. True to his alliances and his training, Henry wrote pamphlets supporting the theology of the church and burned the writings of Martin Luther. The Pope felt that such devotion should be recognized and gave Henry VIII the title "Defender of the Faith" — a title still used at the coronation of British monarchs.

After many years of marriage, Queen Catherine had produced only one possible heir to the throne, and that heir, Mary Tudor, was not a male. Because the English court lacked modern medical knowledge, the failure to produce a royal prince was assigned to Catherine, and in the Spring of 1527, Henry asked the Pope for an annulment.

Power politics now became a factor in the drama. Henry had broken an alliance with Charles V, the new Emperor of the Holy Roman Empire, whose realm extended into northern Italy. The papacy was, therefore, under his military control and there was no possibility that Charles V would permit the Pope to annul Henry V's marriage to Catherine of Aragon. Catherine was Charles V's aunt.

The English response was the Reformation House of Commons, which sat from 1529 to 1536, and which extracted not only vast fines from the church provinces of Canterbury and York, but also brought Henry a new title — "supreme lord ... as far as the law of Christ allows, supreme head." Henry was able to get from Commons a document called "Supplications Against the Ordinaries" aimed at the power of church courts. By the end of 1532, the new Archbishop of Canterbury was Henry's friend and supporter, Thomas Cranmer. One month after his appointment, Henry married Ann Boleyn in secret. Queen Catherine's marriage had to be declared invalid by the new Archbishop of Canterbury who determined that there had been a marriage "in fact but not in law." Ann's marriage was then declared valid.

The relationship with Rome, however, was no longer valid. Henry recognized in his own words "No superior in earth, but only God." The new Queen would soon become pregnant and special efforts were required to encourage the birth of a male heir. A magnificent bed, which had been part of a French nobleman's ransom, was brought to the palace and in it was born on September 7, 1533 the future Queen Elizabeth I.

The third of Henry's six wives did in fact produce a son, the future Edward VI, but the young mother, Jane Seymour, whom Henry really loved, died shortly after the birth. He married three more wives before his own death in 1547. The religious reform precipitated by Henry, which had started by his pursuit of passion, became a religious cause. A Great Bible in English was ordered by Henry to be placed in every church in the land. But the cause of Protestantism in England was far from secure. Some of the bloodiest days of the struggle still lay ahead — under the leadership of the children of Henry VIII. This King, who had been so concerned that he would have no child to succeed him, in fact produced three successors to the English crown.

B-3-g (AR)
Groat
Henry VIII

Chart shows different marriages (Catholic and Spanish marked in red)

```
Henry VIII (1509/47)          m                    Catherine of Aragon ①
    Henry VIII      m    Ann Boleyn ②
          Henry VIII      m    Jane Seymour ③
                    Edward VI (1547/53)
                                          Mary I (1553/8)   m   Phillip II (Spain)
    Elizabeth I (1558/1603)
```

Edward VI assumed power as a boy of 10 in 1547. There was, of course, a regent to run the country — Jane Seymour's brother. Within two years, the Reformation was strengthened when Parliament approved a Book of Common Prayer — even as Catholic farmers in southern England were rebelling. Fate intervened to help the Catholic cause. Edward had been a sickly young man and in 1553 he died, to be succeeded by his Catholic half-sister Mary Tudor, the daughter of Henry's first wife, Catherine of Aragon.

B-3-c (AR)
Shilling
Edward VI

So began the reign of Bloody Mary, who as Queen intended to reverse the foreign policy of England abroad to forge an alliance with her Spanish family, and to reverse the religious policy of England at home. She arranged to marry, by proxy, the man who would someday become Philip II, King of Spain, Europe's most Catholic nation. In England, Mary restored Catholic law and repealed all the laws of the Reformation.

There were still powerful English voices opposing her religious policy, and during Mary's last three years on the throne, 300 English Protestants were burned at the stake. These victims included Henry VIII's close friend and advisor, Thomas Cranmer, the Archbishop of Canterbury, and two bishops, Latimer and Ridley. These two in death did more to stir the Protestant opposition than they could possibly have done in

B-1-a (AV)
Fne Sovereign
Elizabeth I

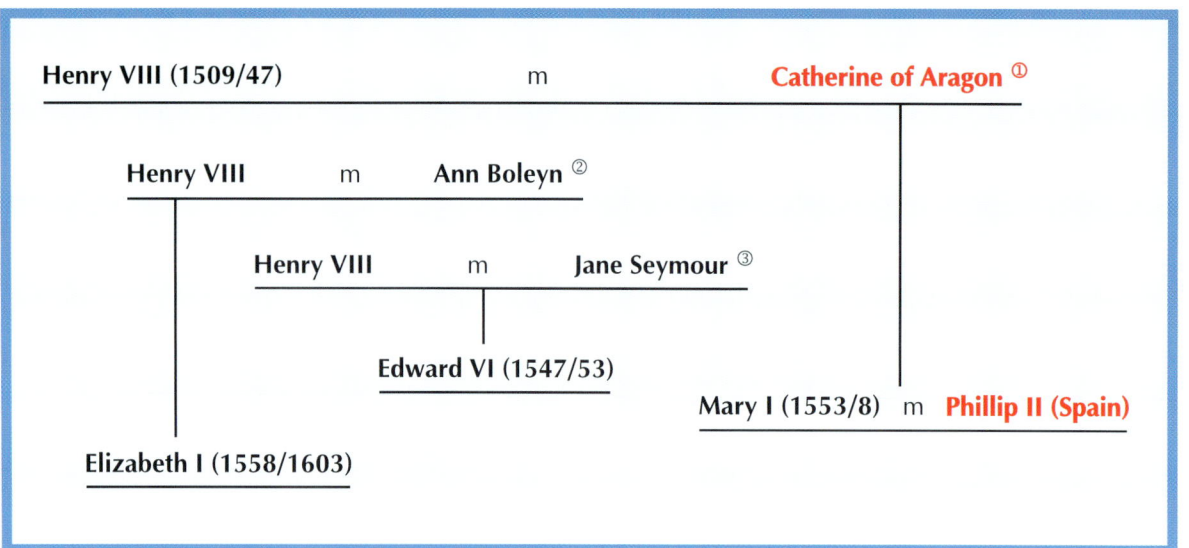

their lives. Latimer, tied to the stake with Ridley, and with the flames rising around them, cried out: "Be of good comfort, Master Ridley. Play the man. We shall this day light such a candle, by God's grace,... as I trust shall never be put out."

Because Mary Tudor had not been successful in linking England's foreign policy to Spain, and because she was unable to conceive, Philip II, now King of Spain, abandoned his royal alliance to her in 1557. Mary died the following year.

Elizabeth I came to the throne at the age of 25 in 1558 and promptly reversed her half-sister's Catholic rulings, making England Protestant by law. Meanwhile, under the leadership of John Knox, Scotland was also becoming Protestant and in 1560, the Treaty of Leith, secured its Presbyterian faith by law. This was all happening around Mary Stuart, Queen of Scotland, who was a Catholic married and allied to the French King Francis II. After Francis died, Mary was imprisoned in Scotland. She managed to escape, however, seeking refuge in Queen Elizabeth's England.

X-x-x (AR)
Testoon
Mary Stuart
(see Glossary)

It turned out to be a safe refuge for many years. Mary Stuart was, however, a magnet for all the forces of the counter-Reformation. In 1585, the Protestant Association brought evidence of a Catholic conspiracy to a review council organized by Francis Walsingham, Elizabeth's chief minister, which found Mary guilty. Two years later, Mary Stuart was escorted by weeping handmaidens to the scaffold where she was to be beheaded. The handmaidens removed her jet black dress and left her standing before the onlookers in a bright crimson bodice and petticoat. Elizabeth was in her palace alone and weeping for the Scottish Queen she had condemned to death.

Much greater trials awaited Elizabeth. In the year 1588, Spain was a great established continental power and also an imperial power with wealth pouring in from its central American possessions, all under control of the House of Aragon. This was the same royal family whose Princess Catherine had been the initial spark of the Reformation as the discarded wife of Henry VIII, and whose present King, Philip II, had been the husband of Mary Tudor. This was, above all, the Catholic royal family of the most Catholic nation of Europe.

Rising against Spain was an aggressive power actively developing a new fleet of warships, pillaging the Spanish galleons and hungry to share Spain's wealth in the new world. That nation, England, was the only Protestant force able to challenge Spain. Philip II recognized the threat. Having been married to Mary Tudor, he claimed the English throne (just as William had done, having married a Saxon Princess). In May of 1588, he dispatched 130 galleons to assault England — the Invincible Armada. Elizabeth mobilized her people and addressed her own forces in a rallying speech at Tilbury, England:

"I know I have the body of a weak and feeble woman but I have the heart and stomach of a king — and a King of England, too."

Elizabeth also had the help of fierce storms which delayed the Armada for two months. When the galleons reached the English Channel, they faced not only 34 very modern warships, holding a total of 6,000 men, but a vast "navy" of more than 150 private vessels. By launching eight fireboats loaded with ammunition, exploding them in the midst of the Armada, and taking advantage of the storm winds in the channel, the English drove the Armada up toward the northern coasts of Britain. Only half of the assault force — 65 vessels — returned to their Spanish ports.

An Armada Medallion was struck to honor the occasion with the legend: "God blew and they were scattered." Following this victory, England became a recognized first-rank power. Religious dissention in England was, for a short time, subdued. And the authority of Parliament rose substantially.

Elizabeth I died in 1603. Henry VIII could not have produced a more successful heir than the woman who had "the heart and stomach of a king." Here was one who truly deserved her title "Defender of the Faith," but it was hardly the faith that the Pope had in mind when he awarded the title to her father.

Elizabeth, known as "the Virgin Queen," had no successors. British monarchs to this day trace their lineage back to her executed foe — Mary Queen of Scots.

Dutch Courage

Philip II, descendant of Isabella, once husband of Bloody Mary Tudor and member of the House of Aragon, was watching a religious dissenter being dragged to the stake when the dissenter cried out to him, "How can you permit me to be burnt?" Philip replied, "I would carry the wood to burn my own son were he as wicked as you."

This was the same King Philip II of Spain who ruled the Netherlands during the latter half of the 16th century and who issued the edicts to "extirpate the sects reprobated by our Holy Mother Church" — in other words, to obliterate the Protestant religions.

William the Silent, the first Prince of Orange, became the center of opposition to these edicts and was joined by many other Dutch nobles, including Catholics who hated the inquisition.

The killing and purification of Holland took place while the population of the country was being reduced to famine and poverty. Queen Elizabeth opened two English ports as a refuge for as many as 30,000 emigrants. Duchess Margaret, the sister of Philip II, was his Regent of the Netherlands for Spain and realized that it was time either to make concessions or to take up arms against the Dutch people.

Count Brederode became the spokesman for the nobles of Holland and on April 3, 1566, was invited to bring the full assemblage of these nobles to be received by the Duchess. The cavalcade of nobles rode through the streets of Brussels, encouraged by wild demonstrations of support and deafening applause as they approached Margaret's palace. At the remarkable meeting that followed in her council chambers, Count Brederode read a petition citing the terrible incidents of judicial murder occurring in the Netherlands, calling for an end to Philip's edicts and an end to the inquisition.

During the reading of the petition, Margaret seemed greatly agitated and at the end sat silent for several minutes — with tears streaming down her face. The Prince of Orange added the point that those present were not rebels, but loyal petitioners, and hoped that an envoy would be appointed to bring the petition to Philip.

At that particular moment, an opportunity existed to spare the country almost half a century of bloodshed and oppression. After the petitioners left, however, one of Duchess Margaret's advisors named Berlaymont made the statement which not only set the course of the nation irrevocably toward war, but also ironically gave the petitioners their war cry. "Madam," he asked, "is it possible that your highness can entertain fears of these beggars?"

Five days later, Count Brederode assembled his 300 noble allies for a luxurious banquet in the town of Culemborg. He did not simply give them the bad news that their petition had failed, he repeated the Berlaymont insult to a room full of outraged aristocrats who proposed forming an alliance — a "Society of Concord." Brederode had a different title in mind. "They call us beggars! Let us accept the name. We will contend with the inquisition ... even till compelled to wear the beggars sack." He circulated a beggar's pouch and a wooden bowl (immediately filled with wine) while the 300 nobles assembled cried out, "Long live the beggars." In the decades to follow, Philip would face the "Wild Beggars" on land and the "Beggars of the Sea" off the coast of Holland. The new confederacy had found its name.

It soon had its costume as well — a gray cloak of coarse material, a common felt hat, a beggar's pouch and a bowl. Around the neck was to be worn a Beggar's Badge showing on its obverse the head of Philip II and on the reverse two clasped hands within a pouch and the inscription, "Faithful to the King (OB) — even to wearing a beggar's sack." (RX)

CHAPTER 9

N-1-x (AV)
Beggar's Badge
(see Glossary)

OB

RX

The ferocity of the war that followed the banquet at Culemborg can be illustrated by the siege of Leyden in 1574. Because Leyden was a coastal town protected by dikes, the sea played a major role in its life. The Dutch were, of course, at home among the shoals and coves of their sometimes submerged land. The sea was also part of their war against Philip II. While Spanish forces held most of the coastline, Prince William held the dikes. He watched anxiously as during the Spring of 1574 the Spanish forces closed a vice around Leyden. By early August the situation in Leyden was desperate. All bread and horse flesh in the town were gone. The trees were stripped of leaves. Dog, cat and rat meat were considered luxuries.

The town was also without any means of securing coinage and, therefore, created its own unique currency. The Dutch creators of this coinage put together twenty-five pages of the Bible which were adhered to each other to form a flat board, from which coins were struck by punch-like cookie cutters.

These coins had printed on the obverse the keys of the city with the inscription "God Save Leyden," and on the reverse the Dutch lion holding aloft the cap of liberty.

OB

N-2-x (made of paper)
The Seige Coin of Leyden
(see Glossary)

The relief of Leyden took place following an ultimatum from the inquisition commander Valdez. The Burgomaster (mayor) of the town gave the response to his own citizens: "Take my body to appease your hunger, but expect no surrender as long as I remain alive." At this stage, the Prince of Orange ordered the dikes to be broken in 16 places — a desperate measure.

Now the Dutch would have an opportunity to use their new navy. On September 28, 1574, its Admiral Boisot released a carrier pigeon advising the inhabitants of Leyden that he was just a few days away. In fact, the water flooding through the broken dikes was still not deep enough to float his ships and no rescue was therefore possible. However, just as gales helped to defeat Philip's Armada 14 years later in his assault on England, a hurricane during the night of October 1st blew the waters of the North Sea across the ruined dikes, more than doubling the water level. There remained fierce opposition by the Spanish, but the Dutch fleet was able to reach the desperate town with sailors throwing bread from every vessel to the famished populous.

RX

Prince William of Orange, now considered the father of his country, was assassinated in 1584. In his last words, he asked God to "have mercy on this poor people." And at the time of his death, he was wearing the Beggar's Badge. His was one of the few in gold. Most of the badges were in lead and copper.

It would be another generation before the Netherlands was finally relieved of the Spanish occupation.

Paradise Removed

The only son of Mary Stuart, the Scottish King James VI, became James I, the successor to Elizabeth and the first King of a united England and Scotland. He was a different kind of ruler — a thinker and scholar. Despite his Catholic mother, he was a Protestant king and a king besieged on all sides. Catholic conspirators almost succeeded in blowing up Parliament. Parliament threatened to exile all who were not members of the established Anglian church. Catholics rebelled in Ireland and this resulted in the first Ulster settlement by Scottish Protestants in North Ireland in the year 1611.

B-3-ee (AR)
Shilling
James I

There was, moreover, a new religious force in English politics. If conscience were the main guide to faith, then it could not only make Protestants out of Catholics, it could also make dissenters out of Anglian Protestants. While Scotland was unifying under the Presbyterian Church, England was discovering many new forms of dissent, and the Puritans would soon become the most important. This vigorous group wanted to simplify Christian belief, ceremony and organization. They sought simple churches with no stained glass and no religious music. They sought an understanding of early Christian religious practice by reading their English Bibles intently. They opposed not only the Pope, but all high-ranking bishops, believing that pastors should be chosen democratically by each church.

The Puritans sought an audience with their new King which was granted at Hampton Court. It appeared at first that they gained little. In fact, what they gained became King James I's most lasting contribution to history. He agreed to produce a new and better English translation of the Bible. This was a demand ideally suited to James' scholarly instincts. In 1604, he assembled hundreds of biblical specialists, including 47 university professors of Greek and Hebrew so that they could painstakingly translate the text into English from the original sources. The King James Bible, completed 13 years later, is still considered to be one of the finest literary works in the English language. Protestant English-speaking people, wherever they lived, had a common link — the King James' Authorized Bible.

The bishops of James' time may have approved their new Bible, but they did not appreciate the rising tide of Puritans who wanted to end their role in the hierarchy. Therefore, they drove many of the toughest dissenters out of the church. In 1607, two Puritan pastors, William Brewster and John Robinson, led thirty-five members of their congregation into exile, where they sought freedom of worship in Leyden, Holland. They did find freedom, but no economic success. In 1620, they joined a group of colonizers from Plymouth, England and set sail for the new world in the 180-ton vessel, the Mayflower. Landing in Cape Cod after a 2½-month journey, they drew up a Compact pledging loyalty to King James and stating as their goal "to plant the first colony in the northern parts of Virginia." When the voyagers learned how far they were from their target, they became in 1627 the chartered "Company of the Mass. Bay in New England." In the following decade, 80,000 Britons would follow them.

Back in the home islands, the British people would face one of the greatest crises of their history. There were any number of reasons why James' son, Charles I, was executed by his own people. He sometimes worked with Parliament, sometimes begged it for money, and at one point dismissed Parliament completely so that for 11 years he reigned as an absolute monarch.

He also infuriated Scotland. In 1637, trying to help the English church, Charles wanted to force the English Prayer Book onto Scotland, his homeland. The Scots, however, regarded this as a step backward

CHAPTER 10

toward Catholicism because of some similarities in the ritual of the Anglican Church. Not only did the effort to impose the Prayer Book fail, but the Scottish people struck back in 1638, issuing a Covenant which stated that the Scots were prepared to die rather than submit to a system they considered to be related to papal rule. Charles' twenty-four year reign from 1625-1649 represented a generation of discord: nationalism vs. Catholicism; high church vs. Presbyterianism; the crown vs. Parliament. In all this turmoil, the Puritans were a rising force now known as Roundheads because, unlike their aristocratic opponents, they cut their hair short.

The year 1642 marked the start of a civil war between the royalty and bishops on one side, against the Puritans, the traders, the dissenters and Parliament on the other. The Roundheads centered their power around London and the Parliament and, with the vast help of London's taxes, were able to raise, train and equip an army of 25,000 men.

There emerged from Parliament one Puritan in particular, the member from Cambridge, Oliver Cromwell, who was considered to be the best military officer to represent parliamentary interests. In the very same year, 1644, in which Charles issued his "Declaration" shilling (honoring the *Protestant Religion*, the *English Law*, the *Freedom of Parliament*),

the military forces under Cromwell, representing Parliament, administered a severe defeat to royalist cavaliers at Maston Moor. One year later, the last decisive battle was fought and won by the Roundheads. Charles, depending on the traditional hostility between Scotland and England, voluntarily put his fate into the hands of his fellow Scots. The English and Scottish authorities, however, reached an agreement and in February 1647 the Scots handed the King over to the Parliamentary Commissioners in return for a guarantee of his safety.

However, Cromwell and the army concluded that there was no way to put the King and the Puritan forces — the New Model Army — on the same team. There was a short struggle between the combined royal bishops, the English navy, the Scottish army and the Welsh against the New Model Army — and the Army won easily. Oliver Cromwell became Dictator of England. On January 30, 1649, King Charles I — never tried in the English courts, but condemned by a Parliamentary commission — was beheaded.

B-3-i (AR)
Shilling
RX: Charles I "Declaration"

B-2-j (AR)
Shilling
Oliver Cromwell

Oliver Cromwell, as head of the Republican Commonwealth, became the uncrowned King of England. He picked his leadership not just for their ability, but for their Puritan devotion.

He forgot his parliamentary origins and ruled as absolutely as any English monarch. His policies inspired either extreme hatred or extreme devotion. One of his most influential devotees was the poet, John Milton, who believed that "tyranny had entered the church" and who attacked all enemies of the Puritans with an acid pen. His poem, Paradise Lost, represented a struggle between Satan and God, and though this allegory was written after Cromwell's death, it may have some relevance to the government of the Commonwealth in which John Milton served as Secretary of the Council of State. Perhaps he was trying to explain Cromwell's abuses when he wrote in *Paradise Lost*:

And with necessity,
The tyrant's plea, excus'd his devilish deeds.

During Cromwell's rule, starting in 1649, he changed England. His rump Parliament issued Puritan decrees. But in 1653, he even closed down his own Parliament, and the country had no representative government at all. Three years later, he was offered the crown and he refused it, accepting instead the title Lord Protector. By now the English people were very tired of Puritan strictures and righteousness. Shakespeare expressed it clearly in the play, *Twelfth Night*:

Sir Toby — "Dost thou think, because thou art virtuous, there shall be no more cakes and ale?"

Cromwell wanted his title to be inherited by his son Richard, but two years following the Lord Protector's death in 1658, the English people did an unexpected thing. They recalled to the throne Charles I's son, Charles II. The Republican and Puritan experiment had failed in its English birthplace. The monarchy had returned.

The restoration of Charles II to the throne took place in 1660. He genuinely wanted to repair the country and, with that in view, issued the Declaration of Breda, expressing conciliation with those who had rebelled against his father (though not forgiving the judges who had condemned him to death). New laws returned to the crown the properties taken by the Commonwealth.

B-2-a (AR)
Half Crown
Charles II

It was in foreign policy that Charles II showed his true Catholic and Stuart nature. Ten years after coming to power, he signed the secret treaty of Dover with Louis XIV of France against the Protestant Dutch. To a great extent this freed him of his dependence on Parliament for huge military budgets. There was one unusual provision in the treaty: Charles agreed to become a Catholic in the future.

When he died in 1685, no subterfuge was needed to return England to Catholic rule. His brother, James II, was a Catholic and within one year issued two Declarations of Indulgence, suspending all of the religious laws against Catholics. The English clergy were ordered to read these decrees from the pulpit and, when seven bishops refused, James brought them to trial. This was, however, a trial by jury and the jury acquitted the bishops. When a son was born to James II, England knew that it would have a second Catholic king as his successor. The result in 1689 was the "Glorious Revolution," which brought to the throne the Dutch William of Orange and his Protestant wife, Mary, who was the daughter of James II. This couple, William and Mary, established a joint rule, and a domestically peaceful one, with an important exception. James II did not go quietly.

-2-e (AR)
Crown
William and Mary

With the help of the Stuart family's traditional French allies, he decided to root out the 74-year-old Ulster settlement in Ireland. He landed on the Irish coast, well supplied with French arms and monies, and secured the whole island to his cause, except for the areas in the north around Londonderry. William of Orange himself led the naval forces which preserved northern Ireland for the crown. More than 300 years later, that struggle between the Orangemen and the Catholics continues down to our own time.

The 600 year-old religious struggle in England, however, was finally over.

* * *

The Puritans meanwhile were finding a new life in the new world. These ardent readers of the bible associated their trials with those of the Old Testament. When they crossed the Atlantic, they were crossing the Red Sea. When they established New England, they were establishing the Promised Land. They named their children Benjamin, Sarah and Rebecca. They built towns of simple wooden salt box houses around pristine, undecorated churches, and with their work ethic, they built a new civilization. Paradise had not been lost. It had been removed across the Atlantic.

So we have come full circle back to America. Can we really know how the colonists felt about church and state? We do know that the devout New Englanders never represented the deity on their coinage. The head of Washington, a non-divine eagle, an Indian or scenes from nature are common features. One typical illustration is the pine tree shilling first struck in 1667 by the settlers of Massachusetts.

U-7-l (AR)
Shilling
Pine Tree

The Puritans were not, of course, the only settlers of the new colonies. Lord Baltimore established a Catholic settlement in Maryland issuing a coin with a legend quoted from Genesis 28: "Increase and multiply." The southern states were settled not so much by those seeking religious refuge as by cavalier adventurers and entrepreneurs. They named the country after the established rulers of the times — Virginia, after the Virgin Queen, Jamestown, Charleston and the Carolinas after the Latin form of the name Charles. God was not totally absent from the southern coinage. A token featuring an elephant on the obverse says on its reverse "God preserve Carolina and the Lord's proprietors."

U-7-hhx (AR)
Shilling
Lord Baltimore

RX: "Increase and Multiply"

Our early settlers were clearly people of faith. They were also — especially many of the northern settlers — people who had been punished for their beliefs by an established religion.

APPENDIX

Special comment with respect to a few coins in this book which relate to their rarity, their provenance, or their publication:

Coin	Subject Matter	Comment	Source
G-3-yy	Anapes	AE Possibly finest quality known in this bronz coin	Bank Leu '00
R-1-aaa	Brutus	AR VF RR	Coin Gallery '59
R-2-k	Hadrian	OR VF + R Head Left	Num Fine Arts '57
R-4-b	Judea Capta	AE EF 16th Century reproduction Giovanni Covino	Stack '52
R-5-o*	Julius Caesar	AV VF RRR	Bank Leu '58
U-7-g	Higley Copper	AE VF RR	Bowers and Merena '84

I-2-w   Mold taken of this coin by Leo Mildenberg for reference in his book "Coinage of the Bar Kochba War."

I-2-p   Mold taken of this coin by Leo Mildenberg for reference in his book "Coinage of the Bar Kochba War."

*See letter with provenance attached from L. Mildenberg on opposite page.

R = Rare   EF = Extra Fine
RR = Very Rare   VF = Very Fine
RRR = Extremely rare

Primary Sources of Coins

Coins of Britain, Greece, Rome and Israel:

    Bank Leu, Zurich, Switzerland
    Coin Galleries, New York, NY
    Numismatic Fine Arts, CA
    Stack's Coin Company, New York, NY

Coins of the American Colonies and the USA:

    Bowers and Merena, Inc., Wolfeboro, NH
    Picker, Long Island, NY
    Stack's Coin Company, New York, NY

Note: *All coins have been enlarged, some two or three times, and some as much as six times or more.*

Provenance of R-5-o

BANK LEU & CO. AG.

BANQUE LEU & CIE S.A.   LEU & CO's BANK LTD.

ANNO 1755

TELEPHON: (051) 23 16 60
POSTCHECK: 80-475

Mr. Henry Pollak
1040 Avenue of the Americas
New York, N.Y. 10018

February 7, 1969

Dear Mr. Pollak

Concerning my health I was in a run of bad luck these last few months and it was quite impossible for me to go abroad. My next trip to the United States is planned for next May. Thank you for your kind invitation.

Of course, I remember the extremely rare Aureus of Caesar (Cohen 33, Sydenham 1329) ex collection Mazzini, plate III, which I sold to you in 1958. As far as I remember there was only one such piece sold during the last decade, i.e. a similar coin of the Ryan collection 1951 in London.

Nowadays, it is very difficult to make out the present market value of this coin: $1150.- may be adequate. Yet a collector who is looking for a Caesar's head of a beautiful style may even pay more. I hope this information will be of any help to you.

I shall call you when I am in New York

Kindest regards,

Sincerely yours,

L. Mildenberg

GLOSSARY

The catalogue references to the coins selected for this book use three characters as follows:

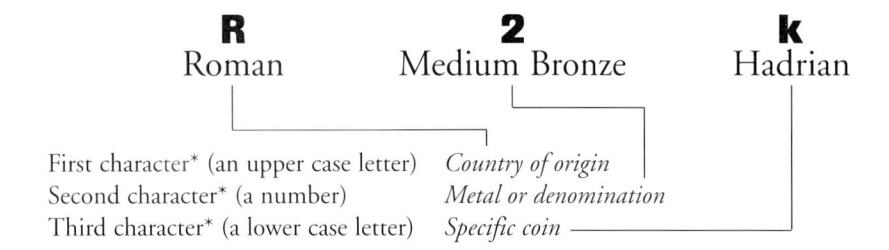

R   **2**   **k**
Roman   Medium Bronze   Hadrian

First character* (an upper case letter) — *Country of origin*
Second character* (a number) — *Metal or denomination*
Third character* (a lower case letter) — *Specific coin*

R-4	Imitations of Roman bronze coins made in the 16th century
N-1-x	Beggar's Badge (photographed — not part of collection)
N-2-x	Seige Coin (photographed — not part of collection)
U-7-hhx	Lord Baltimore (x means photograph of actual coin from Wayte Raymond, 18th. edition)
X-x-x	Photograph of Mary Stuart coin (from Spinks catalog)

Coin Sides:

OB   Face or portrait side of coin
RX   Reverse of coin

Metal Groupings:

AE   Bronze
AR   Silver
AV   Gold
OR   Orichalcum

BIBLIOGRAPHY

Arnold, Edward, *Feudal Britain*, London, 1956.

Banks, Florence Aiken, *Coins of Bible Days*, The MacMillan Co., New York, 1955.

Churchill, Winston, *The Island Race*, Dodd, Mead and Company, London, 1964.

Costain, Thomas, *The Last Plantagenets*, Doubleday, 1962.

Crosby, Sylvester, *Early Coins of America*, self-published, 1875.

Durant, Will, *Caesar and Christ*, Fine Communications, 1994.

Friedberg, Coin and Currency Institute, *Gold Coins of the World* (Series), Clifton, New Jersey, 1958-2001.

Goodacre, Hugh, *Handbook of the Coinage of the Byzantine Empire*, Spink, 1967.

Griffis, William Elliot, *Motley's Dutch Nation, Condensed Version*, Harpers, 1908.

McKisack, *The 14th Century (1307-1399)*, Oxford Press, 1959.

Milne, Sutherland and Thompson, *Coin Collecting*, Oxford University Press, 1950.

Radin, *Jews Among the Greeks & Romans*, Jewish Publication Society, 1916.

Rutherford, Edward, *Sarum*, Ballantine, 1997.

Seltman, Charles, *Masterpieces of Greek Coinage*, Bruno Cassirer/Oxford, 1949.

Synnott, Thomas III, *Thesis*, U.S. Trust Company, 1999.

Taxay, Don, *Counterfeit. Mis-struck and Unofficial U.S. Coins*, Arco Publishing Co., NY, 1963.